Her Spectrum: The Unique Journey of Women and Girls with Autism

Layane Miled

Published by Layane Miled, 2024.

HER SPECTRUM: THE UNIQUE JOURNEY OF WOMEN AND GIRLS WITH AUTISM

First edition. November 28, 2024.

Copyright © 2024 Layane Miled.

ISBN: 979-8230938576

Written by Layane Miled.

Also by Layane Miled

Her Spectrum: The Unique Journey of Women and Girls with Autism

Table of Contents

Introduction

Welcome to *Her Spectrum: The Unique Journey of Women and Girls with Autism.*

In a world where the narrative of autism has often been shaped through the lens of male experiences, this book seeks to illuminate the often-overlooked stories of women and girls on the autism spectrum. You are about to embark on a journey that celebrates individuality, diversity, and resilience—a journey that reveals the unique challenges, strengths, and triumphs of women and girls who navigate life with autism.

For decades, the understanding of autism has been incomplete, leaving many women and girls feeling invisible, misunderstood, or unsupported. Their experiences have often been hidden behind societal expectations, masking behaviors, and diagnostic biases. This book is here to change that. It is a space where their voices are heard, their struggles are acknowledged, and their stories are celebrated.

Whether you are a woman on the spectrum, a parent seeking to better understand your child, a professional working to provide meaningful support, or simply someone curious to learn more, this book is for you. It is designed to provide insight, foster understanding, and inspire action. Each chapter is a step forward in understanding autism through a gendered lens—exploring how it manifests in women and girls, the barriers they face, and the extraordinary ways they rise above them.

This book is not just about challenges; it is also about strength, adaptability, and the incredible potential that lies within every individual on the spectrum. From early childhood to the later years, from navigating education and employment to embracing relationships and personal identity, *Her Spectrum* delves deep into every facet of life, guided by research, expert perspectives, and personal narratives.

Together, we will uncover the invisible layers of autism in women and girls, dismantle stereotypes, and replace them with understanding and empowerment. My hope is that this book serves as a beacon of hope and knowledge—a tool for fostering inclusion, kindness, and progress.

So, welcome. Let's begin this unique journey together. Let's celebrate *Her Spectrum*.

Part I: Understanding Autism in Women and Girls

Autism and Gender: What We Know and What We've Missed

For decades, autism research and diagnosis have predominantly focused on males, leaving women and girls largely underrepresented and misunderstood. This chapter explores the unique ways autism manifests in females, why these differences exist, and how societal norms and biases have shaped the perception of autism. It sets the stage for understanding why many women and girls remain undiagnosed or misdiagnosed and highlights the need for a gender-specific lens in autism research and care.

The historical bias in autism research

The history of autism research is deeply rooted in studies that have primarily focused on males. When Leo Kanner first described autism in 1943, his sample consisted mostly of boys. Similarly, Hans Asperger's work in 1944, which later informed the concept of Asperger's Syndrome, was based on male subjects. This early focus established a precedent that autism is more common in males, a notion that has persisted for decades.

Diagnostic criteria for autism have been largely developed from these male-centric studies. As a result, the tools used to identify autism are often better at detecting the condition in males than in females. This has led to a significant gender gap in diagnosis rates, with estimates suggesting that males are diagnosed with autism at a ratio of approximately 4:1 compared to females.

The underrepresentation of females in autism research has several consequences:

a. **Misdiagnosis and Underdiagnosis**: Many girls and women with autism are either misdiagnosed with other conditions such as anxiety, depression, or eating disorders, or they remain undiagnosed altogether.

b. **Lack of Tailored Support**: Without accurate diagnoses, females may not receive the appropriate interventions and support services they need.

c. **Limited Understanding**: The lack of female representation in research limits our overall understanding of autism and how it affects different genders.

The historical bias highlights the importance of re-evaluating our approaches to autism research and diagnosis to ensure inclusivity and accuracy.

How autism manifests differently in females

Autism can present differently in females, contributing to the challenges in recognition and diagnosis. Understanding these differences is crucial for identifying and supporting women and girls on the spectrum.

a. **Social Camouflaging and Masking**: Many autistic females are adept at mimicking social behaviors to fit in with their peers. This camouflaging can involve rehearsing social interactions, imitating peers, and suppressing autistic traits. While this may help them navigate social situations, it often leads to exhaustion, anxiety, and a delay in diagnosis because their struggles are less visible.

b. **Special Interests**: While autistic males may have intense interests in topics like technology or transportation, females might focus on socially acceptable subjects such as literature, animals, or celebrities. Their interests may not be recognized as atypical, leading to overlooked signs of autism.

c. **Communication Styles**: Autistic girls often have stronger verbal communication skills than boys and may engage more in imaginative play. However, they might still struggle with understanding social nuances, figurative language, and maintaining reciprocal conversations.

d. **Emotional Regulation**: Females on the spectrum may experience heightened emotional sensitivity and may internalize their feelings, leading to co-occurring conditions like anxiety and depression.

e. **Sensory Sensitivities**: Sensory processing differences are common in autism. Females may be particularly sensitive to sounds, textures, or lights but might hide their discomfort to avoid standing out.

f. **Relationships and Social Expectations**: Societal expectations often place pressure on females to be socially adept and empathetic. Autistic girls may feel this pressure acutely, leading them to work harder to fit in, which can mask their autistic traits from parents, teachers, and clinicians.

Understanding these manifestations is essential for parents, educators, and healthcare professionals to recognize autism in females. Early identification allows for timely support, which can significantly improve outcomes.

The importance of gender-specific studies

Addressing the gender disparities in autism requires dedicated research that focuses on females. Gender-specific studies are vital for several reasons:

a. **Improved Diagnostic Criteria**: Research that includes females can lead to the development of diagnostic tools that are sensitive to the ways autism presents in women and girls. This can reduce misdiagnosis and ensure that more females receive accurate assessments.

b. **Tailored Interventions**: Understanding the unique challenges faced by autistic females enables the creation of support programs that address their specific needs, such as coping strategies for social camouflaging and managing co-occurring mental health conditions.

c. **Awareness and Education**: Increased knowledge from gender-specific studies can inform educational materials and training for clinicians, educators, and families, promoting greater awareness and reducing stigma.

d. **Policy and Advocacy**: Data highlighting the experiences of autistic females can influence policy decisions, leading to better resource allocation, support services, and legal protections.

e. **Mental Health Support**: Recognizing the high rates of anxiety, depression, and other mental health issues among autistic females can lead to integrated care approaches that address both autism and mental health.

    f. **Community Building**: Research can help build communities and support networks for autistic women and girls, fostering connections and shared experiences that can alleviate feelings of isolation.

Investing in gender-specific studies not only benefits females on the spectrum but also enriches the overall understanding of autism. It challenges outdated perceptions and encourages a more nuanced view that acknowledges the diversity of the autistic experience.

The Diagnostic Journey

Autism diagnosis in women and girls is often delayed or overlooked due to societal expectations, masking behaviors, and gender-biased diagnostic criteria. This chapter dives deep into the diagnostic process, exploring the challenges unique to females, the impact of delayed diagnosis, and the steps needed to create a more inclusive and accurate system. It aims to empower readers with the knowledge to recognize and advocate for better diagnostic practices.

Challenges in diagnosing girls and women

The process of diagnosing autism in females is complex and often influenced by societal norms, gender expectations, and biases in medical practice. Many girls and women experience significant delays in diagnosis due to a variety of factors:

    a. **Male-Centric Diagnostic Criteria**: Autism diagnostic tools, such as the DSM-5 and ADOS-2, were primarily developed based on research involving males. These tools often emphasize traits that are more prominent in boys, such as overt repetitive behaviors and a narrow range of interests. Females, who may present differently, often slip through the cracks.

    b. **Cultural Expectations**: Girls are often socialized to prioritize relationships, empathy, and compliance, which can mask autistic traits. A girl who struggles to fit in may be perceived as shy or introverted rather than autistic.

c. **Lack of Awareness Among Professionals**: Many clinicians are unfamiliar with the subtle signs of autism in females. They may dismiss symptoms as normal variations in personality or attribute them to other conditions, such as anxiety or depression.

d. **Co-Occurring Conditions**: Many autistic females also experience co-occurring conditions such as ADHD, OCD, or eating disorders. These conditions can overshadow the underlying autism, leading to misdiagnoses or fragmented treatment plans.

e. **Stereotypes About Autism**: Persistent stereotypes, such as the belief that autistic individuals are uninterested in relationships or have poor verbal skills, can further obscure the diagnosis in females, who may exhibit strong communication skills or intense interest in forming connections.

These challenges highlight the urgent need for more inclusive diagnostic approaches that account for the diverse ways autism can manifest across genders.

The impact of masking and camouflaging behaviors

Masking, or camouflaging, is a common coping mechanism among autistic females. It involves suppressing or hiding autistic traits to blend in with social norms, often at great emotional and psychological cost.

a. **What Is Masking?** Masking can take many forms, including imitating social behaviors, rehearsing conversations, and suppressing sensory sensitivities. For instance, a girl might study her peers' mannerisms and replicate them to avoid standing out.

b. **Why Do Females Mask?**
   - **Social Pressure**: Societal expectations for girls to be socially adept and empathetic can drive them to hide their struggles.
   - **Fear of Rejection**: Many autistic females fear being excluded or misunderstood, leading them to mask their true selves.
   - **Desire to Fit In**: The natural human need for belonging can motivate masking, even if it comes at the expense of

authenticity.

c. **Consequences of Masking**:

- **Delayed Diagnosis**: Masking can make it difficult for clinicians to recognize autism, leading to delays in diagnosis.
- **Emotional Burnout**: Suppressing autistic traits requires immense effort and can result in exhaustion, anxiety, and depression.
- **Loss of Identity**: Constantly masking can leave individuals feeling disconnected from their authentic selves.

d. **Breaking the Cycle**: Recognizing and addressing masking behaviors is essential for accurate diagnosis and meaningful support. This includes educating professionals about the subtleties of autism in females and encouraging environments where individuals feel safe to express themselves.

Misdiagnoses and late diagnoses in adulthood

For many autistic women, diagnosis comes late in life, often after years of navigating misdiagnoses and feeling misunderstood. Understanding the patterns of misdiagnosis and the implications of late diagnoses is crucial for improving outcomes.

a. **Common Misdiagnoses**:

- **Anxiety and Depression**: The internalized struggles of autistic females are frequently attributed to anxiety or depression, overlooking the root cause.
- **Personality Disorders**: Conditions like borderline personality disorder (BPD) are sometimes misdiagnosed in autistic women due to overlapping symptoms such as emotional dysregulation.
- **ADHD**: The overlap between ADHD and autism traits can lead to confusion, with many females receiving an ADHD diagnosis without recognizing their autism.

b. **Barriers to Early Diagnosis**:

- **Parental Awareness**: Parents may not recognize subtle signs of autism in their daughters, especially if they do not fit stereotypical depictions of the condition.
- **Educational Systems**: Teachers may misinterpret autistic behaviors as behavioral issues or label them as shyness or defiance.

c. **Life After a Late Diagnosis**:
- **Validation and Relief**: For many women, receiving a diagnosis brings a sense of validation and helps explain years of feeling "different."
- **Identity Reconstruction**: Understanding their autism allows women to embrace their strengths and redefine their self-concept.
- **Access to Support**: A diagnosis can open doors to resources, accommodations, and communities that were previously inaccessible.

d. **The Role of Self-Diagnosis**: Many women turn to self-diagnosis after identifying with autism traits through personal research or community engagement. While self-diagnosis is not a substitute for clinical evaluation, it often serves as a crucial first step in understanding and seeking support.

The Science of Autism in Females

Understanding the science behind autism in females requires a deep dive into the neurological, developmental, and hormonal aspects that contribute to their unique experiences. While autism has traditionally been studied through a male lens, emerging research reveals significant differences in brain structure, hormonal influences, and developmental trajectories in females. This chapter examines these aspects and highlights the gaps in knowledge that still need to be addressed.

Neurological and developmental differences

The brains of autistic females show unique patterns that distinguish them not only from neurotypical females but also from autistic males. These differences play a crucial role in shaping how autism manifests in females.

a. **Brain Structure and Connectivity**:
   Research using brain imaging techniques, such as MRI and fMRI, indicates that autistic females often have distinct patterns of brain connectivity. Key findings include:
   - **Higher Connectivity in Social Brain Regions**: Autistic females may have greater connectivity in regions associated with social cognition, which could explain why they often develop stronger social communication skills than autistic males.
   - **Different Patterns in the Amygdala**: The amygdala, which regulates emotions and social behaviors, may function differently in autistic females, influencing their emotional sensitivity and social interactions.

b. **Developmental Trajectories**:
   Autistic females often exhibit a different developmental timeline compared to males:
   - **Delayed Onset of Challenges**: Many autistic girls appear to develop typical social skills in early childhood but may struggle more noticeably during adolescence, when social expectations become more complex.
   - **Adaptive Learning**: Females are often better at learning to mask their difficulties, which can delay diagnosis and intervention.

c. **Protective Factors**:
   Certain genetic and environmental factors may protect females from more overt presentations of autism:
   - **Genetic Differences**: Some studies suggest that females may require a higher genetic "load" to exhibit autistic traits,

potentially explaining the lower prevalence of autism in females.

- ○ **Social Conditioning**: From a young age, girls are often encouraged to develop social skills and empathy, which may contribute to their ability to adapt and mask challenges.

Hormonal influences on autism traits

Hormonal factors, particularly those related to estrogen and testosterone, can significantly influence autism traits in females.

a. **Prenatal Hormonal Exposure**:
   - ○ **Role of Testosterone**: Higher levels of prenatal testosterone have been linked to increased autistic traits. However, females exposed to similar levels of testosterone may exhibit autism differently, potentially due to the interaction with other genetic or hormonal factors.
   - ○ **Protective Effects of Estrogen**: Estrogen, a predominantly female hormone, may offer some neuroprotective effects that mitigate the expression of autistic traits.

b. **Puberty and Hormonal Shifts**:
   - ○ The onset of puberty often exacerbates sensory sensitivities, emotional regulation issues, and social challenges for autistic females.
   - ○ Hormonal fluctuations during the menstrual cycle can heighten autistic traits, leading to increased anxiety, mood swings, and sensory overload.

c. **Implications for Mental Health**:
   - ○ Hormonal changes throughout life, including during pregnancy and menopause, can significantly impact the mental health of autistic females. These transitions often exacerbate co-occurring conditions such as anxiety and depression.

Current research and gaps in knowledge

Despite advances in understanding autism in females, significant gaps remain in the research landscape.

a. **Underrepresentation in Studies:**
   ◦ Females are often underrepresented in autism research, leading to findings that may not fully capture their experiences. Many studies focus on male-dominated samples, resulting in diagnostic tools and interventions that are less effective for females.
b. **Lack of Longitudinal Studies:**
   ◦ There is a shortage of longitudinal research tracking autistic females across their lifespan. Such studies are essential for understanding how autism evolves in females and how to best support them at different life stages.
c. **Need for Intersectional Approaches:**
   ◦ Autism research often fails to consider how gender intersects with other factors such as race, culture, and socioeconomic status. Addressing these intersections is critical for developing inclusive and effective support systems.

Part II: Autism Across the Lifespan

Infancy and Early Childhood

The earliest stages of life are often where the first signs of autism appear, yet these signs are frequently subtle and easy to overlook in girls. Understanding how autism presents in infancy and early childhood is critical for early diagnosis and intervention, as this period shapes the foundation for lifelong development. In this chapter, we explore the early indicators of autism in girls, the unique differences in play and communication, and the valuable perspectives of parents and caregivers in identifying these traits.

Early signs of autism in girls

Recognizing autism in girls during infancy and early childhood is challenging due to their ability to adapt and blend in with their peers. However, certain traits and behaviors can provide early clues.

a. **Delayed or Atypical Communication Development**:
   - **Speech Delays**: While some autistic girls may have delayed speech, others develop speech at an average pace but struggle with conversational reciprocity, such as taking turns or maintaining eye contact.
   - **Nonverbal Communication**: Girls may use fewer gestures, such as pointing or waving, or may rely heavily on mimicking others' gestures without fully understanding their meaning.

b. **Social Interaction Challenges**:
   - **Preference for Adults or Solitary Play**: Autistic girls might show a preference for interacting with adults rather than peers or engage in solitary play, where they control the narrative of their activities.
   - **Difficulty in Group Settings**: Even in early childhood, girls may feel overwhelmed in group activities, leading them to withdraw or observe rather than participate.

c. **Restricted and Repetitive Behaviors**:
   - **Subtle Special Interests**: Unlike the stereotypical interests in trains or technology seen in boys, girls' interests might be more socially acceptable, such as an intense focus on dolls, animals, or fantasy worlds.
   - **Repetitive Movements**: Behaviors like hand-flapping or toe-walking may occur but are often dismissed as quirks or phases.

d. **Sensory Sensitivities**:
   - Autistic girls may react strongly to certain textures, sounds, or lights. For instance, they might avoid wearing certain fabrics or cover their ears during loud events.

Differences in play, communication, and social interaction

Play and social behaviors are often the areas where autism in girls manifests uniquely. Understanding these differences can help caregivers and educators identify signs of autism early.

a. **Play Patterns**:
  - **Imaginative Play**: Many autistic girls engage in imaginative play, which can appear typical at first glance. However, their play may involve repetitive scenarios or a focus on specific themes, such as role-playing the same story repeatedly.
  - **Preference for Familiarity**: They may prefer structured, predictable play environments and resist changes in their routines.

b. **Peer Relationships**:
  - Girls often attempt to connect with peers but may struggle with the nuances of friendship, such as understanding unspoken rules or managing group dynamics.
  - They might exhibit behaviors like following peers rather than initiating activities, which can lead to misunderstandings or exclusion.

c. **Communication Styles**:
  - Autistic girls might display an advanced vocabulary for their age but struggle with nonverbal cues, sarcasm, or abstract concepts.
  - They may prefer talking about their interests in detail, sometimes without noticing whether the listener is engaged.

Parental and caregiver perspectives

Parents and caregivers play a pivotal role in identifying early signs of autism, as they observe their child's behaviors and development firsthand. Their insights often provide the context needed for accurate diagnosis and support.

a. **Recognizing Subtle Signs**:
  - Many parents notice that their daughters are "different" but

may struggle to articulate how. They might describe their child as unusually quiet, shy, or particular about routines.

b. **Navigating Misconceptions**:
   - Caregivers often encounter resistance when raising concerns about their child's development, as girls' behaviors are frequently dismissed as personality traits or developmental delays that will "catch up" over time.

c. **Seeking Support**:
   - Parents who suspect autism may face challenges in accessing diagnostic evaluations, especially if professionals are unfamiliar with how autism presents in girls. Advocating for assessments and early interventions is crucial.

d. **Building Resilience**:
   - Caregivers of autistic girls often develop a deep understanding of their child's strengths and challenges. Their insights can guide the development of supportive environments at home and in educational settings.

Adolescence: The Hidden Challenges

Adolescence is a transformative period filled with rapid physical, emotional, and social changes. For autistic girls, this stage can present unique challenges that are often misunderstood or overlooked. As they navigate puberty and the complexities of teenage social dynamics, many autistic girls face increased pressures to conform, leading to heightened masking behaviors. Additionally, they may be more susceptible to mental health concerns such as anxiety, depression, and eating disorders. This chapter delves into these hidden challenges, offering insights into how they impact autistic girls and strategies to support them during this critical phase of life.

Coping with puberty and hormonal changes

Puberty marks the onset of significant hormonal shifts that affect the body and mind. For autistic girls, these changes can be particularly overwhelming due to heightened sensory sensitivities and difficulties with emotional regulation.

a. **Physical Changes and Sensory Sensitivities**
   - **Increased Sensory Overload**: The physical developments during puberty—such as growth spurts, changes in body shape, and the onset of menstruation—can intensify sensory experiences. For instance, the feeling of new clothing against the skin, the discomfort of bras, or the sensation of menstrual pads can be distressing.
   - **Managing Menstruation**: The onset of menstruation introduces new sensory and practical challenges. Autistic girls may find it difficult to adjust to the sensations associated with menstrual cramps, the use of sanitary products, and the unpredictability of menstrual cycles.
   - **Body Awareness**: Changes in proprioception (the sense of body position) during growth spurts can affect coordination and increase clumsiness, leading to frustration or embarrassment.

b. **Emotional and Hormonal Fluctuations**
   - **Heightened Emotions**: Hormonal changes can amplify emotions, making it harder for autistic girls to regulate feelings such as anger, sadness, or excitement. This heightened emotional state can exacerbate existing challenges with emotional processing.
   - **Anxiety and Uncertainty**: The unpredictability of bodily changes may lead to increased anxiety. Autistic girls often prefer routine and predictability, so unexpected developments can be particularly distressing.
   - **Communication Difficulties**: Expressing feelings about these changes can be challenging, especially if the girl has

difficulty identifying or articulating her emotions.

c. **Social Implications of Puberty**
   - **Peer Comparison**: As peers undergo puberty at different rates, autistic girls may compare themselves to others, leading to feelings of inadequacy or alienation if they perceive themselves as different.
   - **Navigating Sexual Development**: Understanding the implications of sexual maturation can be confusing. Topics like sexuality, consent, and relationships require nuanced understanding, which may be challenging for autistic individuals.

d. **Strategies for Support**
   - **Education and Preparation**: Providing clear, factual information about what to expect during puberty can reduce anxiety. Visual aids, social stories, and step-by-step guides can be effective tools.
   - **Sensory-Friendly Products**: Offering a variety of menstrual products (e.g., different types of pads, tampons, menstrual cups) and comfortable clothing options can help manage sensory sensitivities.
   - **Emotional Support**: Encouraging open communication about feelings and providing reassurance can help autistic girls navigate emotional fluctuations.
   - **Professional Guidance**: Consulting healthcare professionals who understand autism can ensure that medical advice is tailored to the individual's needs.

Social pressures and the rise of masking behaviors

During adolescence, social dynamics become increasingly complex. Autistic girls often feel pressure to conform to societal expectations, leading to an increase in masking behaviors—suppressing or hiding autistic traits to fit in.

a. **Understanding Masking**

- **Definition**: Masking involves mimicking social behaviors, adopting mannerisms, and rehearsing responses to appear neurotypical.
- **Reasons for Masking**: The desire to be accepted by peers, avoid bullying, or meet adult expectations can motivate autistic girls to mask their authentic selves.

b. **Consequences of Masking**

- **Emotional Exhaustion**: Constantly monitoring and adjusting behavior is mentally draining, leading to fatigue and burnout.
- **Loss of Identity**: Prolonged masking can make it difficult for individuals to understand their true selves, contributing to low self-esteem.
- **Delayed Diagnosis**: Effective masking may prevent others from recognizing autistic traits, delaying access to support and accommodations.

c. **Social Challenges**

- **Peer Relationships**: Interpreting social cues, understanding sarcasm, and navigating group dynamics can be challenging, leading to misunderstandings or social isolation.
- **Bullying and Exclusion**: Autistic girls may be more vulnerable to bullying due to perceived differences, further reinforcing the need to mask.
- **Online Interactions**: The rise of social media introduces new complexities, such as interpreting online communication and managing cyberbullying.

d. **Supporting Authenticity**

- **Encouraging Self-Acceptance**: Promoting environments where autistic girls feel safe to express themselves without judgment can reduce the need for masking.
- **Social Skills Training**: Providing guidance on social norms and communication can help autistic girls navigate social situations more comfortably.

- **Peer Support Groups**: Connecting with other autistic individuals can foster a sense of belonging and validation.

e. **Educating Peers and Educators**
- **Awareness Programs**: Implementing programs in schools to educate students about autism can promote understanding and inclusivity.
- **Teacher Training**: Equipping educators with strategies to support autistic students can create a more accommodating learning environment.

Mental health concerns: anxiety, depression, and eating disorders

Adolescence is a critical period for mental health, and autistic girls are at an increased risk for developing co-occurring mental health conditions.

a. **Prevalence and Risk Factors**
- **Anxiety Disorders**: High levels of anxiety are common due to sensory overload, social challenges, and changes in routine.
- **Depression**: Feelings of isolation, bullying, and difficulties in self-expression can contribute to depression.
- **Eating Disorders**: Autistic girls may develop disordered eating patterns related to sensory sensitivities, a need for control, or body image issues.

b. **Understanding Eating Disorders in Autistic Girls**
- **Sensory-Based Eating Issues**: Preferences or aversions to certain textures, flavors, or colors can limit food choices.
- **Ritualistic Behaviors**: Strict routines around eating times, food presentation, or order of consumption may be present.
- **Interoception Difficulties**: Challenges in recognizing internal body cues, such as hunger or fullness, can affect eating habits.

c. **Challenges in Diagnosis and Treatment**
- **Overlapping Symptoms**: Symptoms of autism and mental

health conditions can overlap, making diagnosis complex.

- ○ **Communication Barriers**: Difficulties in expressing emotions may hinder the identification of mental health issues.
- ○ **Stigma and Misunderstanding**: Misconceptions about autism can lead to underestimation of mental health concerns.

d. **Strategies for Mental Health Support**

- ○ **Early Intervention**: Regular mental health screenings can help identify issues promptly.
- ○ **Tailored Therapies**: Therapeutic approaches should consider autism's impact, utilizing techniques like cognitive-behavioral therapy adapted for autistic individuals.
- ○ **Multidisciplinary Approach**: Collaboration among healthcare providers, educators, and families ensures comprehensive support.

e. **Promoting Well-being**

- ○ **Developing Coping Skills**: Teaching stress management techniques, such as mindfulness or relaxation exercises, can enhance resilience.
- ○ **Building Support Networks**: Encouraging connections with understanding peers, mentors, or support groups can provide emotional relief.
- ○ **Positive Reinforcement**: Recognizing strengths and achievements boosts self-esteem and motivation.

Adulthood: Navigating New Roles

Adulthood brings a new set of challenges and opportunities for autistic women as they strive for independence, build relationships, pursue careers, and set personal goals. The transition into adult life can be both empowering and overwhelming, especially for those who may have been undiagnosed or misdiagnosed in earlier years. This chapter explores the journey of autistic women in adulthood, focusing on establishing routines, navigating personal and professional relationships, and understanding the profound impact that undiagnosed autism can have on their lives.

Finding independence and establishing routines

Achieving independence is a significant milestone for any adult, but for autistic women, it often requires additional planning and support. Establishing routines and managing daily tasks are essential components of independent living, and understanding how to tailor these to individual needs can make the process smoother.

a. **Understanding Independence**
   - **Defining Personal Independence**: Independence doesn't mean doing everything alone; it means having control over one's life choices and decisions. It's about knowing when to ask for help and when to rely on oneself.
   - **Assessing Individual Needs**: Recognize personal strengths and challenges. Some tasks may come easily, while others might require assistance or adaptation.
b. **Establishing Daily Routines**
   - **Importance of Structure**: Routines provide predictability, which can reduce anxiety and improve time management.
   - **Creating a Schedule**: Use planners, calendars, or digital apps to organize daily activities. Break tasks into manageable steps and set reminders.
   - **Flexibility Within Routine**: While structure is helpful, it's also important to build in flexibility to handle unexpected

changes without significant distress.

c. **Developing Life Skills**

- **Household Management**: Skills like cooking, cleaning, and laundry are essential. Start with simple tasks and gradually increase complexity.
- **Financial Literacy**: Learn budgeting, bill payment, and saving. Tools like budgeting apps or financial counseling can be beneficial.
- **Health and Self-Care**: Prioritize physical and mental health through regular exercise, balanced nutrition, and stress management techniques.

d. **Navigating Transportation**

- **Public Transportation**: Familiarize yourself with local transit systems. Practice routes during less busy times to build confidence.
- **Driving**: If appropriate, consider learning to drive. Understand that sensory sensitivities might affect driving comfort and safety.
- **Alternative Options**: Ride-sharing services, biking, or walking can also be viable transportation methods.

e. **Accessing Support Services**

- **Professional Assistance**: Occupational therapists can help develop strategies for daily living skills.
- **Community Resources**: Local organizations may offer classes or support groups focused on independent living skills.
- **Assistive Technology**: Utilize apps and devices designed to aid in organization, communication, and task management.

f. **Overcoming Challenges**

- **Executive Functioning Difficulties**: Use checklists, timers, and visual aids to assist with planning and organization.
- **Sensory Sensitivities**: Create a comfortable living environment by controlling lighting, noise levels, and

textures in your space.

- ◦ **Emotional Regulation**: Practice mindfulness, deep-breathing exercises, or other relaxation techniques to manage stress.

Relationships, careers, and personal goals

Building meaningful relationships, pursuing a fulfilling career, and setting personal goals are integral aspects of adult life. Autistic women may face unique obstacles in these areas but can achieve success with the right strategies and support.

a. **Navigating Personal Relationships**
   - ◦ **Friendships**:
     - ▪ **Finding Common Interests**: Joining clubs, groups, or online communities related to personal interests can facilitate connections with like-minded individuals.
     - ▪ **Maintaining Friendships**: Regular communication and planned activities can help sustain relationships. Be open about communication preferences.
   - ◦ **Family Relationships**:
     - ▪ **Setting Boundaries**: Clearly communicate personal needs and limits to family members.
     - ▪ **Seeking Understanding**: Educate family about autism to foster a supportive environment.
b. **Romantic Relationships**
   - ◦ **Dating**:
     - ▪ **Understanding Social Cues**: Social stories or role-playing can help in recognizing and responding to romantic signals.
     - ▪ **Online Dating**: Provides an opportunity to connect with others at a comfortable pace. Be cautious and prioritize safety.
   - ◦ **Communication**:
     - ▪ **Expressing Emotions**: Practice articulating feelings and needs clearly.
     - ▪ **Active Listening**: Focus on understanding your partner's

perspective and responding thoughtfully.

- ○ **Disclosure of Autism**:
  - ▪ **When to Share**: Deciding when to disclose is personal. Some choose to share early to ensure understanding, while others wait until they feel secure.

c. **Career Development**

- ○ **Identifying Strengths and Interests**:
  - ▪ **Career Assessment**: Use tools or work with a career counselor to identify suitable career paths.
  - ▪ **Leveraging Skills**: Focus on roles that utilize attention to detail, pattern recognition, or specialized knowledge.
- ○ **Job Search Strategies**:
  - ▪ **Resume Building**: Highlight relevant skills and experiences. Consider including volunteer work or personal projects.
  - ▪ **Interview Preparation**: Practice common interview questions and develop strategies to manage anxiety.
- ○ **Workplace Accommodations**:
  - ▪ **Understanding Rights**: Familiarize yourself with laws like the Americans with Disabilities Act (ADA) that protect against discrimination.
  - ▪ **Requesting Accommodations**: This might include flexible scheduling, modified workspaces, or written instructions.

d. **Workplace Challenges**

- ○ **Social Dynamics**:
  - ▪ **Understanding Workplace Culture**: Observe and learn about company norms and expectations.
  - ▪ **Professional Relationships**: Establish clear communication with colleagues and supervisors.
- ○ **Managing Sensory Overload**:
  - ▪ **Workspace Modification**: Use noise-canceling headphones, adjust lighting, or take short breaks as needed.
  - ▪ **Stress Management**: Incorporate relaxation techniques into the workday.

e. **Setting Personal Goals**

- Goal-Setting Techniques:
    - **SMART Goals**: Create Specific, Measurable, Achievable, Relevant, and Time-bound goals.
    - **Prioritization**: Focus on what is most important and break larger goals into smaller, actionable steps.
- **Staying Motivated**:
    - **Tracking Progress**: Use journals or apps to monitor achievements.
    - **Reward Systems**: Celebrate milestones to maintain motivation.
- **Overcoming Obstacles**:
    - **Flexibility**: Be willing to adjust goals as circumstances change.
    - **Seeking Support**: Don't hesitate to ask for help from mentors, friends, or professionals.

The impact of undiagnosed autism on adult women

For many women, autism remains undiagnosed until adulthood, which can profoundly affect various aspects of life.

a. **Challenges of Late or Missed Diagnosis**
   - **Identity and Self-Understanding**:
       - **Feeling Different**: Many women sense they are different but can't pinpoint why, leading to confusion or frustration.
       - **Masking**: Years of camouflaging autistic traits can result in exhaustion and loss of self.
   - **Mental Health Implications**:
       - **Anxiety and Depression**: Persistent stress from navigating a neurotypical world without support can lead to mental health issues.
       - **Misdiagnoses**: Symptoms may be incorrectly attributed to other conditions, delaying appropriate interventions.

b. **Professional and Personal Implications**
   - **Career Challenges**:
       - **Employment Stability**: Difficulties with social interactions or

executive functioning can impact job performance.

- **Underemployment**: Skills and talents may be overlooked, leading to jobs that don't match capabilities.

- **Relationship Struggles**:
  - **Communication Barriers**: Misunderstandings can strain relationships with friends, family, and partners.
  - **Isolation**: Feeling disconnected may lead to withdrawal from social activities.

c. Benefits of Receiving a Diagnosis in Adulthood

- **Validation and Relief**:
  - **Understanding Experiences**: A diagnosis can explain past difficulties and provide a sense of relief.
  - **Reducing Self-Blame**: Recognizing that challenges are related to autism, not personal failures.

- **Access to Resources**:
  - **Support Services**: Eligibility for accommodations, therapies, and support groups.
  - **Community Connection**: Opportunities to connect with others who share similar experiences.

d. Navigating Life Post-Diagnosis

- **Embracing Neurodiversity**:
  - **Self-Acceptance**: Recognize and appreciate unique perspectives and abilities.
  - **Advocacy**: Share experiences to raise awareness and promote acceptance.

- **Building Support Networks**:
  - **Professional Support**: Engage with therapists or coaches specializing in autism.
  - **Peer Support**: Join groups or forums for autistic adults.

e. Strategies for Moving Forward

- **Continued Learning**:
  - **Education**: Read books, attend workshops, or take courses on autism and related topics.
  - **Skill Development**: Pursue interests and hobbies that

enhance skills and bring joy.

- ○ **Setting New Goals**:
  - ▪ **Personal Growth**: Focus on areas of personal interest or areas you wish to improve.
  - ▪ **Career Advancement**: Consider additional training or education to pursue desired career paths.
- ○ **Self-Care Practices**:
  - ▪ **Mindfulness and Relaxation**: Techniques to manage stress and promote well-being.
  - ▪ **Healthy Lifestyle**: Maintain a balanced diet, exercise regularly, and ensure adequate sleep.

Later Years: Aging and Autism

As autistic women enter the later stages of life, they encounter unique challenges and opportunities that differ from those experienced in earlier years. Aging brings about physical, emotional, and social changes that can impact their well-being and quality of life. This chapter explores the specific needs of autistic women as they age, examines common health challenges and comorbidities, and discusses the importance of building supportive communities to enhance their aging experience.

Understanding the needs of autistic women as they age

Aging is a natural part of life, but for autistic women, it can present distinct experiences that require careful consideration. Understanding these needs is crucial for providing appropriate support and enhancing their quality of life.

- a. **Physical Changes and Health Care Needs**
  - ○ **Sensory Sensitivities and Aging**: Sensory processing issues may intensify or change with age. For example, increased sensitivity to sounds, lights, or touch can affect daily activities and comfort levels.
  - ○ **Chronic Health Conditions**: Autistic women may be at higher risk for certain health conditions, such as

autoimmune disorders, gastrointestinal issues, or cardiovascular diseases. Regular medical check-ups and preventive care become increasingly important.

- **Mobility and Physical Functioning**: Age-related changes in mobility may require adaptations in living environments, such as installing assistive devices or modifying homes for accessibility.

b. **Cognitive Changes**

- **Executive Functioning**: Difficulties with planning, organization, and multitasking may become more pronounced, impacting daily routines and independence.
- **Memory and Processing Speed**: Some autistic women may experience changes in memory or cognitive processing, necessitating strategies to manage these shifts.

c. **Emotional and Mental Health**

- **Anxiety and Depression**: Lifelong challenges with mental health may persist or intensify, influenced by factors like retirement, loss of loved ones, or changes in living situations.
- **Adjustment to Life Transitions**: Significant life changes, such as moving to assisted living facilities or adapting to new social roles, can be particularly stressful.

d. **Social Needs and Isolation**

- **Maintaining Social Connections**: As social circles change due to retirement or relocation, maintaining friendships and community involvement is essential to prevent isolation.
- **Communication Challenges**: Continued difficulties with social communication may hinder the formation of new relationships or engagement in community activities.

e. **Access to Appropriate Services**

- **Healthcare Accessibility**: Navigating the healthcare system can be complex, especially when providers lack understanding of autism in older adults.
- **Support Services**: Access to services tailored for older

autistic individuals may be limited, highlighting the need for advocacy and resource development.

f. **Financial Planning and Security**
- ○ **Retirement Planning**: Managing finances for retirement requires careful planning, especially for those who may have had interrupted careers or limited employment opportunities.
- ○ **Accessing Benefits**: Understanding and applying for benefits, pensions, or assistance programs can be challenging without support.

Health challenges and comorbidities

Autistic women may face specific health challenges as they age, influenced by both autism-related factors and general aging processes.

a. **Physical Health Concerns**
- ○ **Autoimmune Disorders**: Research suggests a higher prevalence of autoimmune conditions, such as rheumatoid arthritis or lupus, among autistic individuals.
- ○ **Gastrointestinal Issues**: Chronic digestive problems may persist or worsen with age, affecting nutrition and overall health.
- ○ **Sleep Disorders**: Sleep disturbances are common and can impact energy levels, mood, and cognitive functioning.
- ○ **Cardiovascular Health**: Sedentary lifestyles or stress-related factors may increase the risk of heart disease.

b. **Mental Health Conditions**
- ○ **Anxiety and Depression**: Ongoing mental health issues may be exacerbated by aging-related stressors or hormonal changes, such as menopause.
- ○ **Risk of Neurodegenerative Diseases**: There is limited research on the prevalence of conditions like Alzheimer's disease in autistic women, but monitoring cognitive health is

essential.

  c. **Sensory and Neurological Changes**

- **Sensory Processing**: Changes in sensory perception can affect balance, coordination, and the ability to engage in daily activities.
- **Neurological Conditions**: Increased risk of conditions like epilepsy may persist into older adulthood.

  d. **Access to Quality Healthcare**

- **Communication with Healthcare Providers**: Difficulties in communicating symptoms or health concerns can lead to underdiagnosis or mismanagement of conditions.
- **Healthcare Provider Awareness**: A lack of understanding about autism in older adults among healthcare professionals can hinder effective care.

  e. **Medication Management**

- **Polypharmacy Risks**: Managing multiple medications increases the risk of interactions and side effects, requiring careful monitoring.
- **Adherence Challenges**: Executive functioning difficulties may affect the ability to follow complex medication regimens.

  f. **Preventive Health Measures**

- **Regular Screenings**: Participation in recommended health screenings (e.g., mammograms, bone density tests) is important but may require support to schedule and attend appointments.
- **Lifestyle Factors**: Encouraging physical activity, balanced nutrition, and stress management contributes to overall health.

Building supportive communities for older autistic women

Creating supportive environments and communities is vital for enhancing the quality of life for autistic women as they age.

a. **Social Support Networks**
   - **Peer Groups**: Connecting with other autistic individuals provides a sense of belonging and understanding.
   - **Intergenerational Relationships**: Engaging with younger generations can offer mutual benefits and reduce feelings of isolation.

b. **Community Programs and Activities**
   - **Accessible Activities**: Programs that consider sensory sensitivities and communication preferences enable participation in social, recreational, and educational activities.
   - **Volunteering Opportunities**: Contributing to the community through volunteer work can provide purpose and social engagement.

c. **Housing and Living Arrangements**
   - **Independent Living**: For those who prefer to live independently, access to supportive services that assist with daily tasks is important.
   - **Assisted Living Options**: Facilities that understand and accommodate autistic individuals can offer a safe and comfortable environment.
   - **Cohousing Communities**: Alternative living arrangements that foster community support may be appealing.

d. **Advocacy and Awareness**
   - **Education for Service Providers**: Training for healthcare professionals, caregivers, and social service providers on the needs of older autistic women improves the quality of care.
   - **Policy Development**: Advocating for policies that address the specific needs of aging autistic populations ensures access to necessary resources.

e. **Family and Caregiver Support**
   - **Caregiver Education**: Providing information and training to family members or caregivers enhances their ability to

support effectively.

- ◦ **Respite Services**: Access to respite care helps prevent caregiver burnout and ensures continuous support.

f. **Technology and Assistive Devices**

- ◦ **Communication Tools**: Utilizing technology to aid communication can reduce barriers and increase independence.
- ◦ **Safety and Monitoring Systems**: Devices that assist with medication reminders, emergency alerts, or daily planning can enhance safety.

g. **Mental Health Support**

- ◦ **Counseling Services**: Access to mental health professionals who understand autism can help address emotional challenges.
- ◦ **Support Groups**: Participating in groups focused on mental health or specific interests fosters connection and shared experiences.

Part III: Social and Personal Dimensions of Life

Social Relationships and Friendships

Building and maintaining social relationships can be both rewarding and challenging for autistic women and girls. While friendships offer connection and support, navigating the complexities of social interactions often requires understanding and strategies tailored to their unique experiences. This chapter explores the unique social challenges faced by autistic females, provides guidance on building and maintaining meaningful connections, and offers strategies for fostering inclusion and understanding in various social settings.

Unique social challenges faced by autistic women

Autistic women and girls often experience social interactions differently from their neurotypical peers. Recognizing these unique challenges is essential to providing appropriate support and fostering genuine connections.

a. **Difficulty Reading Social Cues**
   - **Nonverbal Communication**: Autistic females may struggle with interpreting body language, facial expressions, and gestures. This can lead to misunderstandings in conversations, as they might not pick up on cues that indicate sarcasm, humor, or emotional states.
   - **Tone of Voice**: Subtleties in tone, such as irony or teasing, can be confusing. This may result in taking comments literally or missing underlying meanings.

b. **Navigating Social Norms and Expectations**
   - **Unwritten Rules**: Social interactions often involve unwritten rules that are intuitive to neurotypical individuals but can be puzzling to autistic women. Understanding when to speak, how close to stand, or how to join a conversation may not come naturally.
   - **Changing Dynamics**: Social norms can vary between different groups or settings, adding complexity to social navigation.

c. **Masking and Camouflaging**
   - **Suppressing Authentic Behaviors**: To fit in, many autistic women learn to mask their natural responses, mimicking others to appear neurotypical. This can be mentally exhausting and lead to a loss of identity.
   - **Impact on Mental Health**: Prolonged masking is associated with increased anxiety, depression, and burnout, as it requires constant effort to maintain a facade.

d. **Sensory Sensitivities**
   - **Overstimulation**: Sensory sensitivities to light, sound,

touch, or smell can make social environments like parties, concerts, or crowded places overwhelming.

- ○ **Withdrawal from Social Situations**: To cope with sensory overload, autistic women may avoid certain settings, which can limit social opportunities.

e. **Fear of Rejection and Past Experiences**

- ○ **Bullying and Exclusion**: Negative experiences, especially during formative years, can lead to reluctance in forming new relationships due to fear of being hurt or misunderstood.
- ○ **Trust Issues**: Difficulty in interpreting others' intentions may result in wariness or skepticism towards new acquaintances.

f. **Communication Differences**

- ○ **Literal Interpretation**: Autistic women may interpret language literally, missing idioms, metaphors, or jokes, which can create confusion in conversations.
- ○ **Expressing Emotions**: They might find it challenging to articulate feelings or may express them in ways that others perceive as inappropriate.

g. **Time and Energy Management**

- ○ **Social Fatigue**: Interacting socially can be draining, requiring significant mental energy to process conversations and environmental stimuli.
- ○ **Need for Alone Time**: Autistic individuals often need time alone to recharge, which can be misinterpreted by others as disinterest or aloofness.

Building and maintaining meaningful connections

Despite the challenges, autistic women and girls can develop fulfilling friendships with understanding and strategies tailored to their needs.

a. **Finding Like-Minded Individuals**

- ○ **Shared Interests**: Joining clubs, classes, or online communities centered around hobbies (e.g., art, gaming, reading) can facilitate connections with people who share similar passions.

- ○ **Special Interest Groups**: Engaging in groups focused on specific interests can provide a comfortable environment to socialize.

b. **Developing Social Skills**

- ○ **Social Skills Training**: Programs or therapy focusing on social cues, conversation techniques, and nonverbal communication can enhance understanding and confidence.
- ○ **Role-Playing Scenarios**: Practicing conversations and social situations with a trusted person can prepare for real-life interactions.

c. **Effective Communication Strategies**

- ○ **Being Open About Needs**: Sharing preferences with friends (e.g., "I prefer texting over phone calls" or "I might need quiet time during events") can foster mutual understanding.
- ○ **Active Listening**: Demonstrating interest by asking questions and acknowledging what others say strengthens relationships.

d. **Managing Sensory Challenges**

- ○ **Choosing Suitable Environments**: Opt for social settings that are sensory-friendly, such as quiet cafes or outdoor spaces.
- ○ **Using Assistive Tools**: Items like noise-canceling headphones or sunglasses can help manage sensory input during social activities.

e. **Setting Boundaries and Expectations**

- ○ **Clear Communication**: Establishing boundaries regarding personal space, time commitments, and topics of conversation helps prevent misunderstandings.
- ○ **Understanding Personal Limits**: Recognizing signs of social fatigue and taking breaks as needed maintains well-being.

f. **Embracing Authenticity**
- ○ **Being Yourself**: Allowing your genuine interests and personality to shine attracts friends who appreciate you for who you are.
- ○ **Reducing Masking**: Gradually reducing the need to mask in safe environments can alleviate stress and improve mental health.

g. **Maintaining Friendships**
- ○ **Consistency**: Regularly keeping in touch through messages, calls, or planned meet-ups helps sustain relationships.
- ○ **Remembering Special Occasions**: Marking birthdays or significant events in a calendar can aid in acknowledging important moments.

h. **Seeking Support When Needed**
- ○ **Therapeutic Support**: Working with a counselor or therapist experienced in autism can provide personalized strategies for social interactions.
- ○ **Support Groups**: Connecting with other autistic women through groups or forums offers mutual understanding and shared experiences.

Strategies for fostering inclusion and understanding

Creating an inclusive environment requires effort from both autistic individuals and the broader community.

a. **Education and Awareness**
- ○ **Autism Education Programs**: Schools, workplaces, and community organizations can offer training to increase awareness of autism and its diverse presentations.
- ○ **Sharing Personal Stories**: Autistic women sharing their experiences can humanize autism and dispel myths.

b. **Promoting Neurodiversity**
- ○ **Valuing Differences**: Recognizing that neurological

differences contribute to a rich diversity of perspectives and talents.

- ◦ **Inclusive Policies**: Implementing policies that accommodate various communication styles and sensory needs in educational and professional settings.

c. **Encouraging Open Communication**

- ◦ **Asking, Not Assuming**: Encouraging others to ask about preferences and needs rather than making assumptions.
- ◦ **Providing Feedback**: Constructive feedback helps autistic individuals understand social dynamics and adjust if they choose.

d. **Creating Sensory-Friendly Spaces**

- ◦ **Environmental Adjustments**: Modifying lighting, reducing noise levels, and controlling crowd sizes can make events more accessible.
- ◦ **Quiet Zones**: Designating areas where individuals can take a break from sensory stimulation.

e. **Peer Support Programs**

- ◦ **Buddy Systems**: Pairing autistic individuals with supportive peers who can assist with social navigation.
- ◦ **Mentorship Opportunities**: Connecting with mentors who understand autism provides guidance and encouragement.

f. **Addressing Bullying and Discrimination**

- ◦ **Zero-Tolerance Policies**: Establishing and enforcing policies against bullying in schools and workplaces.
- ◦ **Conflict Resolution Training**: Teaching strategies to manage and resolve conflicts constructively.

g. **Family and Community Involvement**

- ◦ **Parental Support**: Families educating themselves and advocating for their autistic members fosters a supportive home environment.
- ◦ **Community Engagement**: Participation in community events promotes visibility and normalizes neurodiversity.

h. **Utilizing Technology**
- ◦ **Social Media and Apps**: Online platforms can facilitate connections and provide alternative means of communication.
- ◦ **Assistive Communication Devices**: Tools that aid in expressing thoughts and feelings can bridge communication gaps.

Pregnancy, Parenting, and Family Life

Embarking on the journey of pregnancy and parenting is a profound experience filled with anticipation, joy, and a myriad of challenges. For autistic women, this journey can be uniquely shaped by their sensory perceptions, communication styles, and ways of interacting with the world. Understanding these distinctive experiences is crucial not only for the mothers themselves but also for their families, healthcare providers, and support networks. This chapter delves into the experiences of autistic women during pregnancy and motherhood, explores strategies for balancing sensory needs with parenting responsibilities, and offers guidance on supporting children, whether they are autistic or neurotypical.

Experiences of autistic women during pregnancy and motherhood

Pregnancy and motherhood bring about significant physical, emotional, and social changes. For autistic women, these changes can interact with their autistic traits in ways that are both challenging and enriching. Recognizing and understanding these experiences can help in providing appropriate support and fostering a positive parenting journey.

a. **Pregnancy: Navigating Physical and Sensory Changes**
- ◦ **Sensory Sensitivities**: Pregnancy often intensifies sensory experiences due to hormonal changes. Autistic women may find that their usual sensory sensitivities become more pronounced. For instance, they might experience heightened sensitivity to smells, tastes, touch, or sounds.

- **Smell and Taste**: Increased sensitivity to odors can lead to nausea or discomfort. Foods that were previously acceptable may become intolerable, affecting nutrition.
- **Touch and Proprioception**: The physical changes of a growing body may lead to discomfort with clothing or physical contact. Understanding and adapting to these changes is essential.
- **Managing Sensory Overload**:
  - **Environment Control**: Creating a comfortable environment with controlled lighting, sounds, and smells can help manage sensory overload.
  - **Communication with Healthcare Providers**: Expressing sensory needs to doctors and midwives can lead to more accommodating care during prenatal visits and delivery.

b. **Emotional and Social Challenges**
- **Processing Emotions**: Pregnancy involves a range of emotions, from excitement to anxiety. Autistic women may process these emotions differently, sometimes finding it challenging to identify or express how they feel.
  - **Alexithymia**: Difficulty in recognizing and articulating emotions can make it hard to seek support when needed.
  - **Strategies**:
    - **Journaling**: Writing down feelings and experiences can help in processing emotions.
    - **Therapy**: Engaging with a therapist who understands autism can provide tools to navigate emotional changes.
- **Social Expectations and Interactions**:
  - **Prenatal Classes**: These classes can be overwhelming due to group interactions. Alternatives include online courses or one-on-one sessions.
  - **Family and Friends**: Well-meaning advice and expectations from others may add pressure. Setting boundaries and communicating preferences is important.

c. **Healthcare Interactions**
   - **Communicating Needs**: Clearly expressing preferences and concerns to healthcare providers ensures better care.
     - **Birth Plans**: Creating detailed birth plans that include sensory preferences can guide healthcare teams during delivery.
   - **Advocacy**:
     - **Support Persons**: Having a trusted individual present during appointments and delivery can help in communication and decision-making.
     - **Educating Providers**: Sharing information about autism can enhance understanding and accommodations.

d. **Motherhood: Adjusting to New Roles**
   - **Routine Changes**: The arrival of a baby disrupts established routines, which can be stressful for autistic mothers who rely on predictability.
     - **Creating New Routines**: Establishing flexible yet structured routines for feeding, sleeping, and caregiving can provide a sense of control.
   - **Sensory Challenges with Infants**:
     - **Crying and Noise**: Babies' cries can be distressing due to auditory sensitivities.
       - **Strategies**:
         - **Noise-Reducing Devices**: Using earplugs or noise-canceling headphones (when safe) can reduce discomfort.
         - **Soothing Techniques**: Learning effective soothing methods for the baby can minimize prolonged crying.
     - **Physical Contact**: Constant touching and holding may be overwhelming.
       - **Alternatives**:
         - **Baby Carriers**: Using carriers or slings can facilitate bonding while keeping hands free.

- - **Shared Caregiving**: Involving partners or family members to share physical caregiving tasks.
  - **Breastfeeding vs. Bottle Feeding**:
    - **Sensory Preferences**: Breastfeeding may present challenges due to tactile sensitivities.
    - **Making Informed Choices**: It's important to choose feeding methods that work best for both mother and baby without guilt or external pressure.

e. **Emotional Well-being and Mental Health**
  - **Postpartum Depression and Anxiety**:
    - **Higher Risk**: Autistic women may be at increased risk due to sensory overload, lack of sleep, and hormonal changes.
    - **Signs to Watch For**: Persistent sadness, withdrawal, excessive worry, or changes in appetite.
    - **Seeking Help**: Early intervention with mental health professionals is crucial.
  - **Self-Care**:
    - **Importance of Rest**: Prioritizing sleep and rest when possible.
    - **Personal Time**: Finding moments for hobbies or relaxation to recharge.

f. **Social Support and Community**
  - **Connecting with Other Mothers**:
    - **Autism-Friendly Groups**: Joining support groups for autistic mothers can provide understanding and shared experiences.
    - **Online Communities**: Virtual connections can offer flexibility and reduce social pressures.
  - **Family Involvement**:
    - **Delegating Tasks**: Accepting help from partners, family, and friends to alleviate stress.
    - **Communication**: Clearly expressing needs and boundaries to those offering support.

g. **Embracing Strengths**
  - **Attention to Detail**: Autistic mothers may excel in noticing

subtle cues from their babies, such as recognizing specific needs based on cries or behaviors.

- ◦ **Consistency**: Providing a stable and predictable environment can be beneficial for child development.
- ◦ **Honesty and Authenticity**: Modeling genuine interactions teaches children about sincerity and acceptance.

Balancing sensory needs with parenting responsibilities

Balancing personal sensory needs with the demands of parenting requires strategies that accommodate both the mother's well-being and the child's care. Understanding how to manage sensory sensitivities while fulfilling parenting roles is key to a harmonious family life.

a. **Identifying Sensory Triggers**
   - ◦ **Self-Awareness**: Recognize specific sensory inputs that cause discomfort or stress.
      - ▪ **Common Triggers**: Loud noises, certain textures, strong smells, visual clutter.
   - ◦ **Monitoring Reactions**: Keeping a journal of sensory experiences and reactions can help in anticipating and managing triggers.
b. **Creating a Sensory-Friendly Home Environment**
   - ◦ **Visual Organization**:
      - ▪ **Decluttering**: Keeping spaces tidy reduces visual overstimulation.
      - ▪ **Soothing Decor**: Using calming colors and minimalistic designs.
   - ◦ **Auditory Adjustments**:
      - ▪ **Soundproofing**: Using rugs, curtains, or acoustic panels to dampen noise.
      - ▪ **White Noise Machines**: Masking disruptive sounds with consistent background noise.
   - ◦ **Tactile Considerations**:
      - ▪ **Comfortable Clothing**: Choosing fabrics that are pleasing to

touch for both mother and child.

- **Adaptable Baby Gear:** Selecting items like strollers or carriers that meet sensory comfort levels.

c. **Implementing Sensory Management Strategies**
  - **Scheduled Breaks:**
    - **Quiet Time:** Incorporating periods of reduced sensory input throughout the day.
    - **Mindfulness Practices:** Engaging in deep breathing, meditation, or gentle exercise.
  - **Sensory Tools:**
    - **Fidget Devices:** Using stress balls or other tools to manage sensory needs.
    - **Weighted Blankets:** Providing calming deep pressure input during rest times.
  - **Adaptive Parenting Techniques:**
    - **Sensory Play:** Engaging in activities that are enjoyable for both mother and child, such as water play or tactile games.
    - **Flexible Routines:** Allowing for adjustments in schedules to accommodate sensory needs.

d. **Communicating Needs to Family Members**
  - **Open Dialogue:**
    - **Explaining Sensory Challenges:** Helping partners and family understand the impact of sensory overload.
    - **Collaborative Problem-Solving:** Working together to find solutions that support the mother's needs.
  - **Setting Boundaries:**
    - **Limiting Overcommitment:** Being selective about social engagements or activities that may be overwhelming.
    - **Designating Personal Space:** Establishing areas in the home where the mother can retreat if needed.

e. **Parenting Techniques That Support Sensory Needs**
  - **Routine Establishment:**
    - **Predictability:** Creating consistent daily schedules can reduce anxiety for both mother and child.

- **Visual Aids**: Using calendars or charts to outline activities.
  - **Positive Discipline**:
    - **Clear Communication**: Providing straightforward instructions and expectations to children.
    - **Understanding Behaviors**: Recognizing that children's actions may also be influenced by their sensory experiences.
- f. **Seeking External Support**
  - **Professional Assistance**:
    - **Occupational Therapy**: Working with therapists who specialize in sensory integration can offer personalized strategies.
    - **Counseling**: Mental health professionals can assist in coping with stress and developing resilience.
  - **Community Resources**:
    - **Parenting Classes**: Participating in programs designed for parents with sensory sensitivities.
    - **Support Groups**: Connecting with other autistic parents for shared advice and encouragement.

Supporting children with or without autism

Whether raising autistic or neurotypical children, autistic mothers bring unique perspectives and strengths to parenting. Understanding how to support children effectively involves recognizing their individual needs and fostering an environment of growth and acceptance.

- a. **Understanding Child Development**
  - **Awareness of Milestones**:
    - **Monitoring Progress**: Keeping track of developmental stages helps in identifying any areas where the child may need additional support.
    - **Avoiding Comparisons**: Recognizing that each child develops at their own pace.
  - **Educational Resources**:
    - **Parenting Books and Websites**: Accessing reliable

information on child development and parenting strategies.

- **Professional Guidance**: Consulting pediatricians or child development specialists when concerns arise.

b. **Supporting Neurotypical Children**
- **Communication Styles**:
  - **Adapting Language**: Ensuring that communication is age-appropriate and understandable.
  - **Active Listening**: Encouraging children to express themselves and acknowledging their feelings.
- **Encouraging Independence**:
  - **Problem-Solving Skills**: Teaching children to think critically and make decisions.
  - **Responsibility**: Assigning age-appropriate tasks to build confidence.
- **Building Emotional Intelligence**:
  - **Emotion Identification**: Helping children recognize and label their emotions.
  - **Empathy Development**: Modeling empathetic behaviors and discussing others' perspectives.

c. **Supporting Autistic Children**
- **Shared Experiences**:
  - **Understanding Challenges**: Autistic mothers may have personal insight into their children's experiences.
  - **Advocacy**: Navigating the education system and accessing services may be more intuitive.
- **Tailored Support Strategies**:
  - **Sensory Accommodations**: Creating environments that consider both the mother's and child's sensory needs.
  - **Communication Methods**: Utilizing alternative communication techniques if needed, such as visual supports or assistive technology.
- **Intervention Programs**:
  - **Early Intervention**: Engaging in therapies that support the child's development.

- **Collaborative Approach**: Working with educators and therapists to create consistent support across settings.

d. Balancing Individual Needs within the Family

- **Family Dynamics**:
  - **Inclusivity**: Ensuring that all family members feel valued and heard.
  - **Equal Attention**: Balancing time and resources among children with varying needs.
- **Managing Conflicting Sensory Needs**:
  - **Compromise Strategies**: Finding solutions when family members have different sensory preferences (e.g., using headphones for differing noise levels).
  - **Designated Spaces**: Creating areas in the home tailored to specific sensory needs.

e. Promoting Positive Relationships

- **Sibling Bonds**:
  - **Fostering Connection**: Encouraging activities that siblings can enjoy together.
  - **Education**: Teaching neurotypical siblings about autism to promote understanding and acceptance.
- **Extended Family Involvement**:
  - **Inclusive Activities**: Planning family events that accommodate everyone's needs.
  - **Education and Awareness**: Informing relatives about autism and sensory sensitivities to enhance support.

f. Preparing for School and Social Integration

- **Education Choices**:
  - **School Selection**: Considering educational environments that align with the child's needs.
  - **Individualized Education Programs (IEPs)**: Advocating for accommodations and supports in school.
- **Social Skills Development**:
  - **Structured Social Opportunities**: Participating in clubs or groups with shared interests.

- **Social Stories and Role-Playing**: Teaching social norms and expectations through practice.

g. **Self-Care and Modeling Healthy Behaviors**
  - **Leading by Example**:
    - **Healthy Habits**: Demonstrating good nutrition, exercise, and stress management.
    - **Emotional Regulation**: Showing effective ways to cope with frustration or anxiety.
  - **Acknowledging Limitations**:
    - **Accepting Imperfection**: Recognizing that it's okay not to have all the answers.
    - **Seeking Help**: Knowing when to reach out for professional support.

Part IV: Education, Employment, and Life Skills

Education: Supporting Girls in the Classroom

Education is a fundamental pillar in the development of every child, providing not only academic knowledge but also socialization and personal growth opportunities. For autistic girls, the classroom environment can present unique challenges and opportunities that differ from those of their neurotypical peers and even autistic boys. Recognizing and addressing the distinct needs of autistic girls in educational settings is crucial for their academic success and overall well-being. This chapter explores how to identify the unique needs of autistic girls in schools, overcome barriers to learning and participation, and implement effective strategies for educators and parents to support these students.

Recognizing the unique needs of autistic girls in schools

Understanding how autism manifests differently in girls is the first step toward providing effective support in educational settings. Autistic girls may exhibit traits that are less overt or stereotypical compared to boys, making it challenging for educators to identify their needs.

a. **Subtle Presentation of Autism in Girls**
  - **Social Camouflaging and Masking**: Autistic girls often engage in masking behaviors, consciously or unconsciously mimicking social behaviors to blend in with peers. This can include copying speech patterns, gestures, and social routines.
    - **Impact on Identification**: Masking can make autistic traits less apparent, leading to underdiagnosis or misinterpretation of behaviors as mere shyness or anxiety.
    - **Emotional Toll**: Sustained masking can result in significant emotional exhaustion and stress, affecting the girl's mental health and academic performance.
  - **Special Interests with Social Acceptability**: While autistic boys might have intense interests in areas like trains or technology, girls may focus on socially accepted subjects such as literature, animals, or popular culture.
    - **Overlooked Signs**: Educators might not recognize these focused interests as a sign of autism because they align with common interests among neurotypical girls.

b. **Communication Styles**
  - **Advanced Vocabulary and Language Skills**: Some autistic girls may exhibit strong verbal abilities, which can mask underlying difficulties with social communication.
    - **Pragmatic Language Challenges**: Despite strong vocabulary, they might struggle with the pragmatic aspects of language, such as understanding idioms, sarcasm, or implicit social rules.
  - **Nonverbal Communication Difficulties**: Challenges with eye contact, facial expressions, and body language may be subtle but present, affecting peer interactions.

c. **Social Interaction Patterns**
  - **Preference for One-on-One Interactions**: Autistic girls may prefer interacting with one or two trusted friends rather than participating in larger group activities.
    - **Misinterpretation**: This preference might be seen as introversion rather than a sign of social communication

differences.

- **Challenges with Peer Relationships**: Navigating the complexities of friendships, particularly during adolescence, can be difficult.
  - **Bullying and Exclusion**: Autistic girls may be more vulnerable to relational bullying, such as exclusion or gossip, due to difficulties in interpreting social cues.

d. **Sensory Sensitivities**
- **Environmental Overload**: Bright lights, loud noises, and crowded classrooms can be overwhelming.
  - **Behavioral Manifestations**: Sensory overload might lead to withdrawal, apparent inattentiveness, or meltdowns, which can be misunderstood by educators.
- **Clothing and Textures**: Discomfort with certain fabrics or clothing tags can cause distraction or distress.

e. **Academic Performance**
- **Perfectionism and Anxiety**: High expectations for themselves may lead to excessive stress over assignments and tests.
  - **Fear of Failure**: This can result in avoidance behaviors or reluctance to participate in class.
- **Executive Functioning Challenges**: Difficulties with organization, time management, and initiating tasks may impact academic success.
  - **Mislabeling**: These challenges might be misconstrued as laziness or lack of motivation.

f. **Co-occurring Conditions**
- **Mental Health Issues**: Increased risk of anxiety, depression, and eating disorders.
  - **Need for Integrated Support**: Addressing co-occurring conditions is essential for overall well-being and academic engagement.

g. **Cultural and Societal Factors**
- **Gender Expectations**: Societal norms regarding how girls should behave

can pressure autistic girls to conform, further masking their needs.

- **Educator Awareness**: Understanding these pressures helps in creating a supportive environment that allows for authentic expression.

Overcoming barriers to learning and participation

Identifying the barriers that hinder autistic girls' educational experiences enables educators and parents to implement strategies that promote inclusion and success.

a. **Environmental Adjustments**
   - **Sensory-Friendly Classrooms**: Modify the classroom to reduce sensory overstimulation.
     - **Lighting**: Use natural light when possible or install dimmable lights.
     - **Noise Reduction**: Incorporate sound-absorbing materials and establish quiet zones.
     - **Seating Arrangements**: Allow flexible seating options to accommodate comfort and focus.
   - **Visual Supports**: Utilize visual schedules, checklists, and cues to aid understanding and predictability.
     - **Benefits**: Helps with transitions, reduces anxiety, and supports executive functioning.
b. **Individualized Education Plans (IEPs) and 504 Plans**
   - **Assessment and Identification**: Early and accurate assessments are crucial.
     - **Collaboration**: Involve multidisciplinary teams, including psychologists, special educators, and speech-language therapists.
   - **Goal Setting**: Develop clear, achievable goals tailored to the student's strengths and needs.
     - **Academic Accommodations**: Extended time on tests, modified assignments, and alternative assessment methods.
     - **Social and Emotional Support**: Include goals for social skills

development and coping strategies.

c. **Social Integration**

  - **Peer Support Programs**: Implement buddy systems or peer mentoring.

    - **Fostering Friendships**: Encourages inclusive interactions and reduces isolation.

  - **Social Skills Training**: Provide explicit instruction on social norms and communication.

    - **Role-Playing and Modeling**: Use practical scenarios to teach and practice skills.

  - **Anti-Bullying Policies**: Enforce clear policies and educate students on empathy and respect.

    - **Reporting Mechanisms**: Ensure students know how to report bullying and feel safe doing so.

d. **Academic Support**

  - **Differentiated Instruction**: Tailor teaching methods to accommodate various learning styles.

    - **Multi-Sensory Approaches**: Engage visual, auditory, and kinesthetic modalities.

  - **Executive Functioning Coaching**: Teach organizational skills, time management, and study strategies.

    - **Use of Technology**: Incorporate apps and tools that assist with planning and note-taking.

  - **Positive Reinforcement**: Provide encouragement and recognize effort and progress.

    - **Feedback**: Offer constructive and specific feedback to guide improvement.

e. **Emotional and Mental Health Support**

  - **Counseling Services**: Access to school counselors or psychologists familiar with autism.

    - **Anxiety Management**: Teach coping mechanisms such as deep breathing, mindfulness, or journaling.

  - **Safe Spaces**: Designate areas where students can go if feeling overwhelmed.

- **Sensory Breaks**: Allow time for students to decompress and regulate.

f. **Communication Between School and Home**
   - **Regular Updates**: Establish consistent communication channels with parents.
     - **Progress Reports**: Share academic and social progress, as well as concerns.
   - **Collaborative Problem-Solving**: Work together to address challenges and adjust strategies.
     - **Parent Involvement**: Encourage participation in school events and decision-making processes.

g. **Professional Development for Educators**
   - **Training on Autism in Girls**: Educate staff on the unique presentations and needs.
     - **Workshops and Seminars**: Provide opportunities for learning about best practices.
   - **Cultural Competency**: Understand how cultural backgrounds may influence the student's experience.
     - **Inclusivity Practices**: Promote a classroom culture that values diversity and individual differences.

Strategies for educators and parents

Effective support for autistic girls in education requires collaboration between educators and parents, utilizing strategies that empower the student and address her individual needs.

a. **Building on Strengths**
   - **Identify Interests and Talents**: Incorporate the student's passions into learning activities.
     - **Engagement**: Using preferred topics can increase motivation and participation.
   - **Strength-Based Approach**: Focus on abilities rather than deficits.
     - **Confidence Building**: Celebrate successes to enhance self-

esteem.

b. **Developing Social Competence**
- **Explicit Teaching of Social Rules**: Break down social expectations into understandable concepts.
  - **Social Stories**: Use narratives to explain social situations and appropriate responses.
- **Group Activities**: Encourage participation in clubs or teams aligned with interests.
  - **Facilitated Interaction**: Provide guidance during group work to support inclusion.

c. **Enhancing Communication Skills**
- **Alternative Communication Methods**: If needed, utilize sign language, picture exchange systems, or communication devices.
  - **Accessibility**: Ensure the student can express needs and participate fully.
- **Pragmatic Language Practice**: Teach nuances of conversation, such as taking turns and staying on topic.
  - **Feedback and Reinforcement**: Offer gentle corrections and praise efforts.

d. **Supporting Emotional Regulation**
- **Recognizing Triggers**: Help the student identify situations that cause stress.
  - **Coping Strategies**: Develop personalized techniques like counting, drawing, or using stress balls.
- **Emotion Identification**: Teach the student to recognize and label emotions.
  - **Empathy Development**: Encourage understanding of others' feelings to navigate social interactions.

e. **Promoting Independence and Self-Advocacy**
- **Decision-Making Opportunities**: Allow the student to make choices about learning activities or assignments.
  - **Empowerment**: Builds confidence and ownership of learning.
- **Self-Advocacy Skills**: Teach how to express needs and seek

help.

- **Role-Playing**: Practice scenarios where the student might need to communicate with authority figures.

f. **Collaboration Between Educators and Parents**
  - **Consistent Strategies**: Align approaches used at school and home for consistency.
    - **Behavior Plans**: Develop joint plans to address specific challenges.
  - **Sharing Resources**: Exchange information on tools, books, or programs that have been effective.
    - **Joint Meetings**: Schedule conferences to discuss progress and adjust plans.

g. **Utilizing Community Resources**
  - **Support Groups**: Connect with local or online communities for additional support.
    - **Networking**: Share experiences and advice with other parents and educators.
  - **Extracurricular Programs**: Enroll the student in activities designed for autistic individuals.
    - **Skill Development**: Provides opportunities for socialization and exploring interests.

h. **Advocacy and Legal Rights**
  - **Understanding Educational Rights**: Familiarize with laws such as the Individuals with Disabilities Education Act (IDEA).
    - **Access to Services**: Ensure the student receives entitled accommodations and support.
  - **Advocacy Training**: Parents and educators can learn how to effectively advocate for the student's needs.
    - **Resource Utilization**: Leverage organizations that specialize in autism advocacy.

Employment: Unlocking Potential in the Workplace

Entering the workforce is a significant milestone that brings both opportunities and challenges. For autistic women, the journey to finding and maintaining employment can be particularly complex due to unique social, sensory, and communication needs. This chapter aims to explore common challenges faced during job searching and retention, provide strategies for advocating for accommodations and workplace inclusion, and share success stories and career inspirations to empower autistic women in unlocking their full potential in the workplace.

Common challenges in job searching and retention

Finding and keeping a job involves navigating various processes, from crafting resumes and attending interviews to adapting to workplace cultures and expectations. Autistic women may encounter specific obstacles in these areas due to differences in social communication, sensory processing, and executive functioning. Understanding these challenges is the first step toward overcoming them.

    a.   **Navigating the Job Search Process**

- **Resume and Cover Letter Writing**

Crafting a resume and cover letter that effectively highlights skills and experiences can be daunting. Autistic women may struggle with:

- **Underestimating Abilities**: Difficulty recognizing or articulating strengths and achievements due to modesty or lack of confidence.
- **Understanding Industry Language**: Challenges in interpreting job descriptions and using appropriate terminology.
- **Organization and Formatting**: Executive functioning difficulties may impact the ability to organize information cohesively.

Strategies:

- **Skill Assessment**: Use self-assessment tools or work with a career counselor to identify strengths and transferable skills.
- **Templates and Guides**: Utilize resume templates and writing guides to structure information effectively.
- **Peer Review**: Seek feedback from trusted individuals to refine documents.

- **Job Applications**

The application process may be overwhelming due to:

- **Complex Forms**: Navigating online application systems with multiple steps and technical glitches.
- **Attention to Detail**: Risk of making errors due to fatigue or misunderstanding instructions.

Strategies:

- **Breaking Down Tasks**: Divide the application process into manageable steps.
- **Assistance Tools**: Use spell-checkers and grammar tools to minimize errors.
- **Time Management**: Allocate specific times for applications to prevent burnout.

a. **Interview Challenges**

- **Social Communication Difficulties**

Interviews often require interpreting social cues, maintaining eye contact, and engaging in small talk, which can be challenging.

- **Anxiety and Stress**: High-pressure situations may exacerbate anxiety, affecting performance.
- **Literal Interpretation**: Difficulty understanding idiomatic

expressions or hypothetical questions.

Strategies:

- **Mock Interviews**: Practice with friends, family, or professionals to become familiar with common questions and scenarios.
- **Preparation**: Research the company and prepare responses to typical interview questions.
- **Disclosure Decisions**: Consider whether to disclose autism to allow for accommodations, such as alternative interview formats.

- **Sensory Sensitivities**
    - **Environment**: Bright lights, noisy waiting areas, or uncomfortable clothing can cause distress.

Strategies:

- **Sensory Management**: Wear comfortable attire, use calming techniques before the interview, and, if necessary, request accommodations.

a. **Workplace Integration and Retention**

- **Understanding Workplace Culture**

Adapting to unwritten rules and social dynamics can be complex.

- **Office Politics**: Difficulty navigating hierarchical structures and informal networks.
- **Teamwork**: Challenges in collaborative projects due to differing communication styles.

Strategies:

- **Mentorship**: Seek out a mentor who can provide guidance on workplace norms.
- **Clear Communication**: Request explicit instructions and feedback

to understand expectations.

- **Sensory and Environmental Factors**
  - **Open Office Layouts**: Noise and lack of privacy may hinder concentration.
  - **Fluorescent Lighting**: Can cause discomfort or headaches.

Strategies:

- **Workspace Adjustments**: Use noise-canceling headphones, request seating in quieter areas, or adjust lighting if possible.
- **Flexible Scheduling**: Explore options for remote work or flexible hours.

- **Executive Functioning Challenges**
  - **Time Management**: Difficulties in prioritizing tasks or meeting deadlines.
  - **Organization**: Keeping track of multiple projects or administrative tasks.

Strategies:

- **Task Management Tools**: Utilize planners, calendars, and apps to organize responsibilities.
- **Regular Check-Ins**: Schedule meetings with supervisors to clarify expectations and progress.

a. **Social Interactions and Networking**

- **Building Professional Relationships**

Forming connections with colleagues can enhance career development but may be challenging due to:

- **Small Talk**: Difficulty engaging in casual conversations.
- **Networking Events**: Overwhelming sensory environments and social demands.

Strategies:

- **Structured Interactions**: Participate in organized group activities or committees with clear objectives.
- **Preparation**: Develop a list of conversation starters or topics of interest.

- **Misunderstandings and Conflicts**
    - **Communication Styles**: Directness may be misinterpreted as bluntness.
    - **Interpreting Feedback**: Difficulty distinguishing between constructive criticism and personal criticism.

Strategies:

- **Communication Training**: Learn about workplace communication styles and adapt as comfortable.
- **Feedback Clarification**: Ask for specific examples to understand feedback fully.

Advocating for accommodations and workplace inclusion

Understanding one's rights and effectively communicating needs are crucial for creating an inclusive work environment. Advocacy involves both self-advocacy and promoting broader organizational change to support diversity and inclusion.

a. Understanding Legal Rights

- **Employment Laws**
    - **Americans with Disabilities Act (ADA)**: Prohibits discrimination based on disability and requires employers to provide reasonable accommodations.
    - **Equal Employment Opportunity Commission (EEOC)**: Enforces laws against workplace discrimination.

Actions:

- **Educate Yourself**: Familiarize with relevant laws and protections.
- **Documentation**: Keep records of communications and any instances of discrimination.

a. Deciding Whether to Disclose Autism

- **Pros of Disclosure**
  - **Access to Accommodations**: Legal right to reasonable adjustments.
  - **Promoting Understanding**: Educating employers and colleagues can foster a supportive environment.
- **Cons of Disclosure**
  - **Stigma and Bias**: Potential for misunderstanding or discrimination.
  - **Privacy Concerns**: Personal information becoming widely known.

Considerations:

- **Personal Comfort**: Weigh the potential benefits against the risks.
- **Selective Disclosure**: Share information with HR or supervisors as needed.

a. Requesting Accommodations

- **Identifying Needs**
  - **Assess Work Environment**: Determine which aspects present challenges.
  - **Specific Requests**: Clearly articulate what accommodations would be helpful.
- **Communication Strategies**
  - **Formal Request**: Submit a written request to HR or a supervisor.
  - **Provide Documentation**: May include a diagnosis or recommendations from a healthcare professional.
- **Examples of Accommodations**
  - **Modified Workspaces**: Quiet areas, partitions, or alternative lighting.
  - **Flexible Scheduling**: Adjusted hours or remote work options.
  - **Communication Adjustments**: Written instructions, visual aids, or

regular meetings for clarification.

a. Promoting Workplace Inclusion

- **Employee Resource Groups (ERGs)**
  - **Creating Communities**: Join or establish groups focused on neurodiversity.
  - **Support and Advocacy**: ERGs can influence policies and raise awareness.
- **Education and Training**
  - **Workshops**: Advocate for training sessions on autism and inclusion.
  - **Awareness Campaigns**: Participate in events that promote understanding.
- **Inclusive Policies**
  - **Recruitment Practices**: Encourage hiring processes that reduce bias, such as skills-based assessments.
  - **Performance Evaluations**: Advocate for clear, objective criteria.

a. Dealing with Discrimination

- **Recognizing Unfair Treatment**
  - **Signs**: Being passed over for promotions, unequal workloads, or exclusion from meetings.
- **Taking Action**
  - **Internal Resolution**: Address concerns with HR or a trusted supervisor.
  - **External Support**: Consult legal professionals or advocacy organizations if necessary.

Success stories and career inspiration

Hearing from autistic women who have navigated the workplace successfully can provide motivation and practical insights. These stories highlight diverse career paths and demonstrate that with the right support and determination, autistic women can thrive professionally.

a. Case Study: Dr. Temple Grandin

- **Background**
    - ◦ **Career**: Renowned animal scientist and professor at Colorado State University.
    - ◦ **Contributions**: Revolutionized livestock handling equipment design, emphasizing animal welfare.
- **Challenges Overcome**
    - ◦ **Communication Barriers**: Utilized visual thinking to innovate in her field.
    - ◦ **Advocacy**: Became a prominent speaker and author on autism, educating others.
- **Lessons Learned**
    - ◦ **Leveraging Strengths**: Used her unique perspective to solve complex problems.
    - ◦ **Persistence**: Overcame skepticism and discrimination through dedication.

a. Case Study: Haley Moss

- **Background**
    - ◦ **Career**: First openly autistic lawyer admitted to the Florida Bar.
    - ◦ **Contributions**: Advocate for disability inclusion and author.
- **Challenges Overcome**
    - ◦ **Academic Hurdles**: Navigated law school with accommodations.
    - ◦ **Professional Integration**: Advocated for herself in the workplace.
- **Lessons Learned**
    - ◦ **Self-Advocacy**: Emphasizes the importance of communicating needs.
    - ◦ **Visibility**: Uses her platform to inspire others and promote inclusion.

a. Diverse Career Paths

- **Technology Sector**
    - ◦ **Roles**: Software developers, data analysts, cybersecurity experts.
    - ◦ **Strengths Utilized**: Attention to detail, pattern recognition, and logical reasoning.
- **Creative Industries**

- ○ **Roles**: Writers, artists, graphic designers, musicians.
  - ○ **Strengths Utilized**: Unique perspectives, creativity, and innovation.
- **Healthcare and Education**
  - ○ **Roles**: Researchers, therapists, educators.
  - ○ **Strengths Utilized**: Empathy, dedication to helping others, specialized knowledge.

a. Strategies from Successful Autistic Women

- **Embrace Individuality**
  - ○ **Authenticity**: Allow your unique traits to shine rather than conforming to neurotypical norms.
  - ○ **Strength-Based Approach**: Focus on what you do well and seek roles that align with your abilities.
- **Continuous Learning**
  - ○ **Professional Development**: Engage in training, certifications, or education to enhance skills.
  - ○ **Adaptability**: Stay open to new experiences and be willing to adjust strategies.
- **Networking**
  - ○ **Building Connections**: Join professional organizations or online communities.
  - ○ **Mentorship**: Seek mentors who understand your journey and can provide guidance.

a. Inspirational Quotes

- **Temple Grandin**: "The world needs all kinds of minds."
- **Haley Moss**: "Being different isn't a bad thing. It means you're brave enough to be yourself."

Life Skills and Independent Living

Life skills and independent living are essential components of personal growth and fulfillment for autistic women and girls. Mastering these skills empowers individuals to navigate daily challenges, build self-confidence, and achieve greater autonomy. This chapter explores strategies for managing daily tasks, achieving financial independence, and effectively navigating a world that often caters to neurotypical norms.

Building self-confidence and managing daily tasks

Developing self-confidence and effectively managing daily tasks are crucial steps toward independent living. Autistic women and girls may face unique challenges in these areas due to differences in executive functioning, sensory processing, and social communication. However, with the right strategies and support, they can build the skills necessary to thrive independently.

a.   **Understanding Self-Confidence**

- **What is Self-Confidence?**

Self-confidence is the belief in one's abilities to accomplish tasks and face challenges. It involves self-assurance in personal judgment, abilities, and power, which can be particularly important when overcoming societal misconceptions about autism.

- **Challenges to Self-Confidence in Autism**
    - **Societal Misunderstandings**: Negative stereotypes and misunderstandings about autism can impact self-esteem.
    - **Past Experiences**: Previous failures or difficulties, especially in social situations, may lead to self-doubt.
    - **Comparison with Neurotypical Peers**: Feeling different or not fitting in can affect confidence levels.

a.   **Strategies for Building Self-Confidence**

- **Recognizing Strengths**
    - ○ **Skill Assessment**: Identify personal strengths, talents, and interests. This could include attention to detail, strong memory, creativity, or specialized knowledge.
    - ○ **Positive Affirmations**: Practice affirming one's abilities and achievements regularly.
- **Setting Achievable Goals**
    - ○ **SMART Goals**: Create Specific, Measurable, Achievable, Relevant, and Time-bound goals to provide clear direction and a sense of accomplishment.
    - ○ **Incremental Steps**: Break larger tasks into smaller, manageable steps to avoid feeling overwhelmed.
- **Celebrating Successes**
    - ○ **Acknowledgment**: Recognize and celebrate achievements, no matter how small.
    - ○ **Reward Systems**: Implement a system of rewards for reaching milestones to reinforce positive behavior.
- **Building a Supportive Network**
    - ○ **Family and Friends**: Surround oneself with supportive individuals who encourage and understand.
    - ○ **Mentors and Role Models**: Seek out individuals who have successfully navigated similar challenges.
- **Self-Care Practices**
    - ○ **Mindfulness and Relaxation Techniques**: Practices such as meditation, deep breathing, or yoga can reduce anxiety and improve self-esteem.
    - ○ **Physical Health**: Regular exercise, sufficient sleep, and a balanced diet contribute to overall well-being.

a. **Managing Daily Tasks**

- **Executive Functioning Skills**

Autistic individuals may experience difficulties with executive functioning, which includes planning, organization, time management, and task initiation.

- **Time Management**
  - Use of Schedules and Planners
    - **Visual Schedules**: Utilize calendars, planners, or digital apps to keep track of appointments, deadlines, and daily routines.
    - **Timers and Alarms**: Set reminders for important tasks or to signal transitions between activities.
  - Prioritization Techniques
    - **To-Do Lists**: Create daily or weekly lists to outline tasks that need to be completed.
    - **Eisenhower Matrix**: Categorize tasks based on urgency and importance to prioritize effectively.
- **Organization**
  - Decluttering Spaces
    - **Minimalism**: Keep living and working spaces tidy to reduce sensory overload and improve focus.
    - **Designated Storage**: Use labeled containers and specific places for items to simplify locating them.
  - Digital Organization
    - **File Management**: Organize digital files and emails into clearly labeled folders.
    - **Password Management**: Use secure password managers to keep track of login information.
- **Task Initiation and Completion**
  - Motivation Techniques
    - **Interest-Based Activities**: Incorporate interests into tasks where possible to increase engagement.
    - **Accountability Partners**: Work with someone who can provide encouragement and check in on progress.
  - Overcoming Procrastination
    - **Five-Minute Rule**: Commit to working on a task for just five minutes to overcome the initial barrier.
    - **Environmental Cues**: Arrange the environment to minimize distractions and prompt action.
- **Adaptive Strategies**

- ○ **Assistive Technology**
    - **Apps and Tools**: Utilize apps designed for people with executive functioning challenges, such as note-taking apps, task managers, or focus enhancers.
    - **Smart Home Devices**: Use technology like smart lights or voice assistants to automate routine tasks.
- ○ **Occupational Therapy**
    - **Professional Support**: An occupational therapist can provide personalized strategies to improve daily living skills.

a. Building Independence in Daily Living

- **Self-Care Skills**
    - ○ **Personal Hygiene**
        - **Routine Establishment**: Create checklists for daily hygiene tasks like showering, brushing teeth, and grooming.
        - **Sensory Considerations**: Choose products that are comfortable and acceptable in terms of texture, scent, and sensation.
    - ○ **Nutrition and Meal Planning**
        - **Simple Recipes**: Start with easy-to-follow recipes to build cooking skills.
        - **Meal Prep**: Plan meals in advance to reduce daily decision-making and ensure a balanced diet.
- **Household Management**
    - ○ **Cleaning Routines**
        - **Scheduled Tasks**: Assign specific chores to certain days to maintain a clean living environment.
        - **Checklists**: Use cleaning checklists to ensure all areas are addressed.
    - ○ **Laundry and Clothing Care**
        - **Simplify Processes**: Use laundry baskets sorted by color to streamline washing.
        - **Clothing Choices**: Opt for easy-care garments that do not require special handling.

- **Transportation Skills**
  - ○ **Public Transportation**
    - ▪ **Route Planning**: Use transit apps to plan trips and track schedules.
    - ▪ **Practice Runs**: Do trial runs during less busy times to become familiar with routes.
  - ○ **Driving**
    - ▪ **Driving Lessons**: Seek instructors experienced in teaching autistic individuals if pursuing a driver's license.
    - ▪ **Alternatives**: Consider biking, walking, or ride-sharing services if driving is not preferable.

Financial independence and budgeting

Achieving financial independence is a critical aspect of adult life. It involves understanding how to manage money, budget for expenses, and plan for the future. For autistic women and girls, developing these skills may require tailored strategies to accommodate different learning styles and challenges with executive functioning.

a. **Understanding Personal Finance**

- **Basic Financial Concepts**
  - ○ **Income vs. Expenses**: Recognize the importance of living within one's means by ensuring expenses do not exceed income.
  - ○ **Needs vs. Wants**: Differentiate between essential expenses (needs) and non-essential purchases (wants).
- **Setting Financial Goals**
  - ○ **Short-Term Goals**: Saving for immediate needs like a new computer or a vacation.
  - ○ **Long-Term Goals**: Planning for education, buying a home, or retirement.

a. **Budgeting Strategies**

- **Creating a Budget**
    - ○ **Track Income and Expenses**
        - ▪ **Income Sources**: Include wages, benefits, or any other sources of money.
        - ▪ **Expense Categories**: Break down expenses into categories such as housing, food, transportation, utilities, and entertainment.
    - ○ **Budgeting Methods**
        - ▪ **Envelope System**: Allocate cash to envelopes for each expense category to control spending.
        - ▪ **50/30/20 Rule**: Allocate 50% of income to needs, 30% to wants, and 20% to savings and debt repayment.
- **Using Financial Tools**
    - ○ **Budgeting Apps**: Utilize apps like Mint, YNAB (You Need A Budget), or PocketGuard to automate tracking and budgeting.
    - ○ **Spreadsheets**: Create customized budgets using spreadsheet software for more control.

a. **Managing Bank Accounts**

- **Checking and Savings Accounts**
    - ○ **Choosing a Bank**: Consider factors like fees, accessibility, customer service, and online banking options.
    - ○ **Understanding Account Features**: Learn about interest rates, minimum balances, and overdraft protection.
- **Online Banking**
    - ○ **Monitoring Accounts**: Regularly check balances and transactions to stay informed.
    - ○ **Automatic Payments**: Set up automatic bill payments to avoid late fees.

a. **Building Credit**

- **Understanding Credit**
    - ○ **Credit Score**: A numerical representation of creditworthiness that affects the ability to borrow money.

- ◦ **Credit History**: Record of borrowing and repayment behaviors.
- **Using Credit Responsibly**
  - ◦ **Credit Cards**
    - ▪ **Choosing a Card**: Select one with favorable terms, low interest rates, and benefits that match needs.
    - ▪ **Payment Practices**: Pay off the balance in full each month to avoid interest and build a positive credit history.
  - ◦ **Loans**
    - ▪ **Types of Loans**: Understand differences between personal loans, student loans, car loans, etc.
    - ▪ **Repayment Plans**: Choose manageable repayment schedules and be aware of interest rates.

a. **Saving and Investing**

- **Emergency Fund**
  - ◦ **Purpose**: Set aside funds to cover unexpected expenses like medical bills or car repairs.
  - ◦ **Goal Amount**: Aim for 3-6 months' worth of living expenses.
- **Long-Term Savings**
  - ◦ **Retirement Accounts**: Consider options like 401(k)s, IRAs, or other retirement savings plans.
  - ◦ **Investments**: Learn basic investing principles if interested, but proceed cautiously and consider professional advice.

a. **Managing Debt**

- **Understanding Debt**
  - ◦ **Types of Debt**: Distinguish between secured (e.g., mortgages) and unsecured debts (e.g., credit cards).
  - ◦ **Interest Rates**: High-interest debts can accumulate quickly, making them a priority to pay off.
- **Debt Repayment Strategies**
  - ◦ **Debt Snowball Method**: Pay off debts starting with the smallest balance to build momentum.

- Debt Avalanche Method: Prioritize debts with the highest interest rates to save money over time.

a. **Financial Education Resources**

- **Workshops and Courses**
    - **Community Programs**: Attend local workshops or classes on personal finance.
    - **Online Courses**: Utilize free or paid online resources to learn at one's own pace.
- **Financial Advisors**
    - **Professional Guidance**: Consult with a financial advisor, especially for complex situations or investment planning.
- **Books and Blogs**
    - **Educational Materials**: Read books or follow blogs focused on personal finance for additional tips and insights.

a. **Overcoming Financial Challenges**

- **Dealing with Impulsive Spending**
    - **Awareness**: Recognize triggers for impulsive purchases, such as stress or sensory seeking.
    - **Delay Techniques**: Implement a waiting period before making non-essential purchases.
- **Advocating for Fair Treatment**
    - **Understanding Rights**: Be aware of consumer protection laws and financial rights.
    - **Seeking Assistance**: Reach out to consumer advocacy groups if facing unfair practices.

Learning to navigate a "neurotypical" world

The world is largely designed with neurotypical individuals in mind, which can present challenges for autistic women and girls. Learning to navigate this environment involves developing strategies to cope with societal expectations, advocating for oneself, and fostering understanding among others.

a. Understanding Neurotypical Norms

- **Social Expectations**
    - **Unwritten Rules**: Recognize that many social norms are implicit and may require observation or inquiry to understand.
    - **Cultural Differences**: Be aware that norms can vary across different cultures and communities.
- **Communication Styles**
    - **Nonverbal Cues**: Learn about body language, facial expressions, and tone of voice that convey meaning beyond words.
    - **Small Talk**: Understand the role of casual conversation in building rapport.

a. Developing Coping Strategies

- **Social Skills Training**
    - **Workshops and Classes**: Participate in programs that teach social interaction skills in a structured environment.
    - **Role-Playing**: Practice social scenarios with friends, family, or therapists to build confidence.
- **Sensory Management**
    - **Preparation**: Plan ahead for sensory challenges by bringing items like earplugs, sunglasses, or fidget tools.
    - **Self-Regulation Techniques**: Employ methods like deep breathing or taking breaks to manage sensory overload.

a. Self-Advocacy

- **Communication**

- - **Expressing Needs**: Clearly articulate personal needs and preferences to others.
  - **Setting Boundaries**: Establish and maintain personal boundaries to ensure comfort and respect.
- **Education**
  - **Informing Others**: Share information about autism when appropriate to foster understanding.
  - **Resource Sharing**: Provide materials or references to help others learn.

a. Building Social Connections

- **Finding Like-Minded Individuals**
  - **Interest Groups**: Join clubs or organizations related to hobbies or passions.
  - **Online Communities**: Participate in forums or social media groups that offer support and connection.
- **Quality Over Quantity**
  - **Meaningful Relationships**: Focus on developing deep, authentic connections rather than a large number of acquaintances.

a. Navigating Public Spaces

- **Understanding Public Etiquette**
  - **Queueing**: Learn the norms around waiting in lines and personal space.
  - **Public Transportation**: Familiarize oneself with the rules and expectations when using buses, trains, or subways.
- **Safety Awareness**
  - **Personal Security**: Be mindful of surroundings and trust instincts if a situation feels unsafe.
  - **Emergency Preparedness**: Know how to respond in emergencies by learning basic procedures.

a. Employment and Education Settings

- **Workplace Adaptation**

- ○ **Professional Conduct**: Understand workplace norms, such as dress codes, punctuality, and communication protocols.
  - ○ **Networking**: Develop skills for professional networking, including attending events and maintaining contacts.
- **Educational Environments**
  - ○ **Classroom Participation**: Learn strategies for engaging in discussions and group projects.
  - ○ **Accessing Accommodations**: Advocate for necessary support services in educational settings.

a. Dealing with Discrimination and Misunderstanding

- **Recognizing Bias**
  - ○ **Subtle Discrimination**: Be aware of microaggressions or subtle forms of prejudice.
  - ○ **Institutional Barriers**: Understand systemic challenges that may exist.
- **Response Strategies**
  - ○ **Assertiveness Training**: Develop skills to assertively address discrimination.
  - ○ **Seeking Support**: Engage with advocacy groups or legal resources if necessary.

a. Embracing Neurodiversity

- **Positive Identity**
  - ○ **Self-Acceptance**: Embrace autism as a valuable aspect of identity.
  - ○ **Community Involvement**: Connect with the neurodiversity movement to promote acceptance and inclusion.
- **Challenging Stereotypes**
  - ○ **Representation**: Share personal stories and experiences to combat misconceptions.
  - ○ **Allyship**: Encourage allies to support neurodiversity initiatives.

Part V: Health, Well-Being, and Self-Advocacy

Physical and Mental Health

Autistic women often face unique physical and mental health challenges that can impact their quality of life. Understanding these concerns is essential for effective self-care, accessing appropriate medical support, and advocating for better health outcomes. This chapter delves into common health issues experienced by autistic women, explores strategies for addressing mental health conditions such as anxiety, depression, and burnout, and examines the barriers to healthcare access along with potential solutions.

Common health concerns in autistic women

Autistic women may experience a range of physical health issues that are either directly related to autism or occur more frequently in the autistic population. Recognizing these common concerns is crucial for timely diagnosis, management, and improving overall well-being.

a. **Gastrointestinal Disorders**

- **Prevalence and Symptoms**
    - **High Occurrence:** Studies have shown that gastrointestinal (GI) issues are more prevalent among autistic individuals, including women.
    - **Common Symptoms:** These can include chronic constipation, diarrhea, abdominal pain, bloating, and gastroesophageal reflux disease (GERD).
- **Potential Causes**
    - **Gut-Brain Axis:** The connection between the gut and the nervous system may contribute to GI issues in autism.
    - **Dietary Factors:** Sensory sensitivities may lead to restrictive eating habits, affecting gut health.
    - **Stress and Anxiety:** Emotional states can exacerbate GI symptoms.
- **Management Strategies**
    - **Medical Evaluation:** Consult a healthcare provider for proper diagnosis

and treatment.

- ◦ **Dietary Adjustments**: Incorporate fiber-rich foods, probiotics, or consider specialized diets under professional guidance.
- ◦ **Stress Reduction**: Techniques like mindfulness or gentle exercise can alleviate symptoms.

a. 2. Sensory Processing Disorders

- **Understanding Sensory Processing**
  - ◦ **Definition**: Difficulty in processing and responding to sensory information from the environment.
  - ◦ **Impact**: Can affect touch, taste, smell, sight, hearing, balance, and body awareness.
- **Manifestations in Daily Life**
  - ◦ **Hyper-Sensitivity**: Over-responsiveness to stimuli such as bright lights, loud noises, or certain textures.
  - ◦ **Hypo-Sensitivity**: Under-responsiveness, seeking intense sensory experiences.
- **Coping Strategies**
  - ◦ **Sensory Diets**: Structured activities that provide the necessary sensory input.
  - ◦ **Environmental Modifications**: Adjusting lighting, reducing noise, and creating sensory-friendly spaces.
  - ◦ **Occupational Therapy**: Working with a therapist to develop personalized strategies.

a. Sleep Disorders

- **Types of Sleep Issues**
  - ◦ **Insomnia**: Difficulty falling or staying asleep.
  - ◦ **Irregular Sleep-Wake Patterns**: Disrupted circadian rhythms leading to inconsistent sleep schedules.
  - ◦ **Restless Leg Syndrome**: Uncomfortable sensations causing an urge to move the legs.
- **Contributing Factors**

- ○ **Sensory Sensitivities**: Discomfort due to bedding textures or environmental noises.
  - ○ **Anxiety and Overthinking**: Racing thoughts preventing relaxation.
  - ○ **Melatonin Production**: Possible differences in melatonin levels affecting sleep regulation.

- **Improving Sleep Hygiene**
  - ○ **Consistent Routine**: Establish regular sleep and wake times.
  - ○ **Sleep Environment**: Create a dark, quiet, and comfortable bedroom.
  - ○ **Limit Stimulants**: Reduce caffeine and electronic device usage before bedtime.
  - ○ **Professional Support**: Seek advice from sleep specialists if necessary.

a. **Hormonal and Reproductive Health**

- **Menstrual Challenges**
  - ○ **Sensory Discomfort**: Pads, tampons, or menstrual cups may cause discomfort due to sensory sensitivities.
  - ○ **Pain Management**: Higher sensitivity to pain can make menstrual cramps more severe.

- **Polycystic Ovary Syndrome (PCOS)**
  - ○ **Increased Prevalence**: Some studies suggest a higher occurrence of PCOS in autistic women.
  - ○ **Symptoms**: Irregular periods, acne, weight gain, and excess hair growth.

- **Menopause**
  - ○ **Intensified Symptoms**: Hot flashes, mood swings, and sleep disturbances may be more pronounced.

- **Managing Hormonal Health**
  - ○ **Medical Consultation**: Regular check-ups with gynecologists to monitor reproductive health.
  - ○ **Pain Relief Options**: Over-the-counter medications or alternative therapies for menstrual discomfort.
  - ○ **Hormone Therapy**: Discuss potential benefits and risks with healthcare providers during menopause.

a. **Chronic Pain and Ehlers-Danlos Syndrome (EDS)**

- **Association with EDS**
  - ○ **Connective Tissue Disorders**: Autistic individuals may have a higher prevalence of conditions like hypermobility EDS.
  - ○ **Symptoms**: Joint hypermobility, chronic pain, and frequent injuries.
- **Impact on Daily Life**
  - ○ **Physical Limitations**: Pain and joint issues can hinder mobility and activities.
  - ○ **Emotional Effects**: Chronic pain may contribute to fatigue and low mood.
- **Management Approaches**
  - ○ **Physical Therapy**: Exercises to strengthen muscles and support joints.
  - ○ **Pain Management Plans**: Working with specialists to control pain levels.
  - ○ **Adaptive Tools**: Using braces or mobility aids as needed.

a. 6. Autoimmune Disorders

- **Higher Risk Factors**
  - ○ **Immune System Differences**: Research indicates a possible link between autism and autoimmune conditions like lupus or rheumatoid arthritis.
- **Symptoms and Detection**
  - ○ **Varied Manifestations**: Symptoms can be widespread and non-specific, making diagnosis challenging.
  - ○ **Regular Screening**: Early detection is key to managing autoimmune diseases effectively.
- **Treatment Strategies**
  - ○ **Medical Management**: Medications to control the immune response.
  - ○ **Lifestyle Adjustments**: Diet, exercise, and stress reduction to support overall health.

a. Neurological Conditions

- **Epilepsy**
  - ○ **Co-Occurrence**: Autistic individuals have a higher incidence of seizure disorders.
  - ○ **Types of Seizures**: May range from absence seizures to generalized tonic-

clonic seizures.

- **Migraine and Headaches**
  - ○ **Sensory Triggers**: Light, sound, or certain foods may precipitate migraines.
  - ○ **Management**: Identifying triggers and using prescribed medications.

Addressing mental health: anxiety, depression, and burnout

Mental health is a critical aspect of overall well-being, and autistic women often face unique challenges in this domain. High rates of anxiety, depression, and autistic burnout highlight the need for targeted support and effective coping strategies.

a. Understanding Anxiety Disorders

- **Prevalence and Presentation**
  - ○ **High Incidence**: Anxiety disorders are common among autistic women due to factors like sensory overload, social challenges, and uncertainty.
  - ○ **Types of Anxiety**: Generalized anxiety disorder, social anxiety disorder, panic disorder, and specific phobias.
- **Contributing Factors**
  - ○ **Sensory Sensitivities**: Overwhelm from environmental stimuli can trigger anxiety responses.
  - ○ **Social Pressures**: Difficulties in social interactions may lead to fear of judgment or rejection.
  - ○ **Change and Uncertainty**: Preference for routine makes unexpected changes stressful.
- **Coping Strategies**
  - ○ **Cognitive Behavioral Therapy (CBT)**: A therapeutic approach to challenge negative thought patterns.
  - ○ **Mindfulness and Relaxation Techniques**: Practices like meditation, deep breathing, and progressive muscle relaxation.
  - ○ **Routine Establishment**: Creating predictable schedules to reduce anxiety.

a. **Addressing Depression**

- **Signs and Symptoms**
  - **Emotional Indicators**: Persistent sadness, hopelessness, and loss of interest in activities.
  - **Physical Symptoms**: Changes in sleep patterns, appetite, and energy levels.
  - **Cognitive Effects**: Difficulty concentrating, making decisions, or remembering details.
- **Risk Factors**
  - **Social Isolation**: Feelings of loneliness due to social difficulties.
  - **Masking Fatigue**: Exhaustion from continual efforts to appear neurotypical.
  - **Unrecognized Autism**: Late or missed diagnoses can contribute to feelings of frustration and self-doubt.
- **Treatment Approaches**
  - **Psychotherapy**
    - **Individual Therapy**: Working with a therapist experienced in autism to explore emotions and develop coping mechanisms.
    - **Group Therapy**: Provides a sense of community and shared experiences.
  - **Medication**
    - **Antidepressants**: May be prescribed to manage symptoms, with careful monitoring for side effects.
  - **Lifestyle Modifications**
    - **Physical Activity**: Regular exercise can improve mood and reduce symptoms.
    - **Social Engagement**: Participating in activities that foster connection.

a. **Recognizing and Managing Autistic Burnout**

- **What is Autistic Burnout?**
  - **Definition**: A state of intense physical, mental, or emotional exhaustion accompanied by reduced ability to cope with daily demands.

- **Distinct from Depression**: While overlapping symptoms exist, burnout is specifically linked to the cumulative effect of navigating a neurotypical world.

- **Causes**
  - **Chronic Stress**: Prolonged exposure to stressors without adequate recovery time.
  - **Masking and Camouflaging**: Continuous effort to hide autistic traits can deplete energy reserves.
  - **Sensory Overload**: Persistent exposure to overwhelming sensory environments.

- **Symptoms**
  - **Increased Sensitivity**: Heightened reactions to sensory input.
  - **Reduced Functioning**: Difficulty with tasks that were previously manageable.
  - **Withdrawal**: Desire to isolate oneself to conserve energy.

- **Recovery Strategies**
  - **Rest and Downtime**: Prioritize rest periods and reduce non-essential activities.
  - **Simplify Routines**: Streamline daily tasks to minimize decision fatigue.
  - **Seek Support**
    - **Professional Help**: Consult mental health professionals familiar with autistic burnout.
    - **Community Support**: Connect with others who understand and can offer empathy.

a. **Co-occurring Mental Health Conditions**

- **Obsessive-Compulsive Disorder (OCD)**
  - **Overlap with Autism**: Repetitive behaviors and routines may be present in both conditions.
  - **Distinguishing Factors**: OCD involves intrusive thoughts and compulsions aimed at reducing anxiety.

- **Eating Disorders**
  - **Anorexia Nervosa and Avoidant/Restrictive Food Intake Disorder (ARFID)**

- **Sensory Influences**: Texture, taste, or smell sensitivities may affect eating habits.
- **Control and Predictability**: Eating patterns may provide a sense of control in an unpredictable world.

- **Attention Deficit Hyperactivity Disorder (ADHD)**
  - **Comorbidity**: Many autistic women also have ADHD, affecting attention and impulse control.
  - **Integrated Treatment**: Addressing both conditions can improve outcomes.

a. **Access to Mental Health Services**

- **Barriers**
  - **Misdiagnosis**: Symptoms may be attributed solely to autism, overlooking mental health conditions.
  - **Lack of Specialist Knowledge**: Therapists may not be trained in working with autistic adults, leading to ineffective treatment.
  - **Communication Challenges**: Difficulty articulating feelings or experiences can hinder therapy.
- **Overcoming Barriers**
  - **Finding the Right Professional**: Seek out practitioners experienced in autism and co-occurring mental health issues.
  - **Advocacy**: Communicate specific needs and preferences to mental health providers.
  - **Teletherapy Options**: Online therapy may provide greater accessibility and comfort.
  -

Accessing healthcare: challenges and solutions

Autistic women often face significant hurdles when seeking healthcare, from communication barriers to sensory challenges within medical environments. Understanding these obstacles and implementing strategies to overcome them is vital for ensuring equitable healthcare access.

a. **Communication Barriers**

- **Challenges**
  - **Expressing Symptoms**: Difficulty in describing symptoms or pain levels accurately.
  - **Understanding Medical Language**: Complex terminology can be confusing.
  - **Interpreting Nonverbal Cues**: Misreading body language or tone from healthcare providers.
- **Solutions**
  - **Preparation**
    - **Symptom Journals**: Keep detailed records of symptoms, triggers, and questions to share during appointments.
    - **Practice Discussions**: Rehearse conversations with a trusted person to gain confidence.
  - **Written Communication**
    - **Bring Notes**: Hand over written summaries to the provider.
    - **Request Written Instructions**: Ask for explanations and care plans in writing.
  - **Support Persons**
    - **Bring an Advocate**: Have a trusted individual accompany you to appointments for support and clarification.

a. **Sensory Challenges in Medical Settings**

- **Environmental Stressors**
  - **Bright Lights**: Fluorescent lighting can be overwhelming.
  - **Noises**: Beeping machines, crowded waiting rooms, and loud conversations.
  - **Physical Sensations**: Uncomfortable seating, medical procedures involving touch.
- **Strategies for Coping**
  - **Scheduling**
    - **Quiet Times**: Book appointments during less busy hours.
    - **Minimal Wait Times**: Request to wait in a quieter area or

outside.

- ◦ **Sensory Tools**
    - ▪ **Bring Comfort Items**: Headphones, sunglasses, fidget devices, or weighted blankets.
    - ▪ **Dress Comfortably**: Wear clothing that is easy to remove for examinations and comfortable to wear.
- ◦ **Communicate Needs**
    - ▪ **Inform Staff**: Let the healthcare team know about sensory sensitivities and how they can help.

a. Misdiagnosis and Diagnostic Overshadowing

- **Understanding the Issue**
    - ◦ **Diagnostic Overshadowing**: Attributing all symptoms to autism, leading to missed or incorrect diagnoses of other health conditions.
    - ◦ **Gender Bias**: Women's symptoms, particularly pain, may be taken less seriously or dismissed.
- **Strategies to Prevent Misdiagnosis**
    - ◦ **Advocate for Thorough Evaluation**
        - ▪ **Persist**: If concerns are not addressed, seek a second opinion.
        - ▪ **Provide Detailed Information**: Offer comprehensive symptom descriptions and history.
    - ◦ **Educate Providers**
        - ▪ **Share Information**: Provide resources on autism in women to healthcare professionals.

a. Navigating the Healthcare System

- **Finding the Right Providers**
    - ◦ **Research**
        - ▪ **Specialist Directories**: Use directories to find providers experienced with autistic patients.
        - ▪ **Recommendations**: Seek suggestions from support groups or online communities.
    - ◦ **Compatibility**

- **Initial Consultation**: Consider scheduling a preliminary meeting to assess comfort levels.

- **Insurance and Costs**
  - **Understanding Coverage**
    - **Review Policies**: Know what services are covered under your insurance plan.
    - **Financial Assistance**: Inquire about payment plans or sliding scale fees.
  - **Advocacy**
    - **Patient Advocates**: Utilize hospital patient advocates for assistance with billing or accessing services.

a. Health Literacy and Self-Education

- **Importance of Health Literacy**
  - **Empowerment**: Understanding health information enables better decision-making.
  - **Compliance**: Increases the ability to follow treatment plans effectively.
- **Improving Health Literacy**
  - **Educational Resources**
    - **Reliable Websites**: Access information from reputable sources like medical institutions or government health departments.
    - **Support Groups**: Learn from others with similar experiences.
  - **Ask Questions**
    - **Clarification**: Do not hesitate to ask providers to explain information in simpler terms.

a. Cultural and Societal Barriers

- **Stigma and Discrimination**
  - **Prejudices**: Negative attitudes toward autism can affect the quality of care.
  - **Intersectionality**: Women of color, LGBTQ+ individuals, and those from marginalized communities may face additional barriers.
- **Advocacy and Awareness**

- ○ **Policy Changes**
  - ▪ **Support Legislation**: Advocate for policies that promote inclusive healthcare practices.
- ○ **Community Engagement**
  - ▪ **Education Initiatives**: Participate in efforts to educate healthcare professionals and the public.

Eating and Sensory Sensitivities

Eating and sensory sensitivities significantly impact the lives of autistic women and girls, influencing their nutritional intake, social interactions, and overall well-being. These challenges often stem from the way sensory information is processed, leading to unique food preferences, aversions, and sometimes disordered eating patterns. This chapter delves into the complexities of food-related challenges and disorders, offers practical strategies for managing sensory processing differences, and shares personal perspectives alongside expert advice to provide a comprehensive understanding of these issues.

Understanding food-related challenges and disorders

Food-related challenges among autistic women and girls are multifaceted, often rooted in sensory sensitivities, rigid routines, and emotional factors. Recognizing and understanding these challenges is essential for promoting healthy eating habits and preventing nutritional deficiencies or the development of eating disorders.

a. **Sensory Processing and Food Preferences**

- **Sensory Sensitivities**
  - ○ **Taste and Texture**: Many autistic individuals have heightened sensitivity to certain tastes and textures. Foods that are too bitter, sour, spicy, or have an unfamiliar texture can be overwhelming.
  - ○ **Smell and Appearance**: The smell or visual appearance of food can influence willingness to eat. Strong odors or foods that look unappealing may be avoided.
  - ○ **Temperature Sensitivity**: Preferences for foods served at specific

temperatures (e.g., only cold foods) can limit dietary variety.

- **Impact on Diet**
  - ○ **Selective Eating**: A limited range of acceptable foods can lead to a restricted diet, potentially causing nutritional imbalances.
  - ○ **Monotropic Interests**: Intense focus on specific foods or food groups, sometimes leading to overconsumption of certain items while neglecting others.

a. Routine and Rituals in Eating

- **Rigid Eating Patterns**
  - ○ **Consistency and Predictability**: A strong preference for routine may manifest in eating the same foods repeatedly or following strict meal schedules.
  - ○ **Food Presentation**: Specific ways of preparing or presenting food (e.g., cutting sandwiches into particular shapes) may be important.
- **Challenges with Change**
  - ○ **Introducing New Foods**: Deviating from established routines or trying unfamiliar foods can cause significant anxiety.
  - ○ **Environmental Factors**: Changes in dining environments, such as eating in a different location or with unfamiliar people, can be distressing.

a. Emotional Factors and Control

- **Anxiety and Food**
  - ○ **Comfort in Control**: Controlling food intake may provide a sense of security in an unpredictable world.
  - ○ **Stress-Related Eating**: Anxiety may lead to overeating or undereating as a coping mechanism.
- **Association with Emotions**
  - ○ **Emotional Avoidance**: Avoiding food may be a way to suppress uncomfortable emotions.
  - ○ **Reward and Punishment**: Using food as a reward or punishment can create unhealthy relationships with eating.

a. **Eating Disorders in Autistic Women**

- **Higher Prevalence**
    - ○ **Anorexia Nervosa**: Characterized by restrictive eating and an intense fear of gaining weight.
    - ○ **Avoidant/Restrictive Food Intake Disorder (ARFID)**: Involves limited food intake due to sensory sensitivities or lack of interest in eating.
- **Contributing Factors**
    - ○ **Perfectionism and Control**: Traits common in autism, such as attention to detail and desire for control, may contribute to the development of eating disorders.
    - ○ **Misdiagnosis and Overlooked Symptoms**: Eating disorders may be misinterpreted as typical autistic behaviors or go unnoticed due to masking.
- **Impact on Health**
    - ○ **Physical Consequences**: Nutritional deficiencies, weakened immune system, and organ damage.
    - ○ **Mental Health Effects**: Increased risk of depression, anxiety, and social isolation.

a. **Social Implications**

- **Social Eating Situations**
    - ○ **Challenges in Social Settings**: Difficulty participating in meals with others due to sensory issues or anxiety.
    - ○ **Peer Pressure**: Feeling pressured to eat certain foods or adhere to social eating norms.
- **Stigma and Misunderstanding**
    - ○ **Judgment from Others**: Unusual eating behaviors may be misunderstood, leading to social stigma.
    - ○ **Lack of Awareness**: Friends, family, and professionals may not recognize the connection between autism and eating challenges.

a. **Importance of Early Recognition and Support**

- **Preventing Long-Term Issues**
    - ○ **Nutritional Health**: Early intervention can prevent serious health consequences.
    - ○ **Emotional Well-Being**: Addressing issues promptly supports mental health and self-esteem.
- **Role of Professionals**
    - ○ **Multidisciplinary Approach**: Collaboration among healthcare providers, nutritionists, therapists, and educators.
    - ○ **Individualized Care**: Tailoring strategies to meet the specific needs of each individual.

Strategies for managing sensory processing differences

Managing sensory processing differences related to eating involves implementing practical strategies that accommodate individual needs while promoting a balanced diet and positive eating experiences. These approaches can be applied at home, in educational settings, and in social environments.

a. Sensory-Friendly Food Exploration

- **Gradual Introduction of New Foods**
    - ○ **Desensitization Techniques**: Slowly introducing new foods by starting with small quantities or combining with preferred foods.
    - ○ **Sensory Play**: Engaging with food through non-eating activities (e.g., touching, smelling) to reduce anxiety.
- **Texture and Flavor Adjustments**
    - ○ **Modifying Food Consistency**: Preparing foods in textures that are more acceptable, such as pureeing or finely chopping.
    - ○ **Flavor Enhancements**: Using mild spices or sauces to alter taste without overwhelming the senses.
- **Visual Appeal**
    - ○ **Presentation**: Arranging food in visually pleasing ways or using colorful plates and utensils.
    - ○ **Food Variety**: Incorporating a range of colors and shapes to make meals more engaging.

a. **Creating a Comfortable Eating Environment**

- **Controlled Sensory Input**
    - **Lighting**: Adjusting the brightness or using natural light to create a calming atmosphere.
    - **Noise Reduction**: Minimizing background noises by turning off appliances or using soft music.
- **Consistent Mealtime Routines**
    - **Predictability**: Establishing regular meal times and routines to provide a sense of security.
    - **Familiar Settings**: Eating in the same location or using the same utensils and dishes.
- **Personal Space**
    - **Seating Arrangements**: Allowing for personal space at the table to reduce sensory overload.
    - **Comfort Items**: Using cushions or weighted lap pads to provide additional comfort.

a. **Involving the Individual in Meal Preparation**

- **Empowerment through Participation**
    - **Cooking Together**: Involving the individual in shopping, meal planning, and cooking to increase acceptance of foods.
    - **Choice and Control**: Allowing them to make choices about what to eat within balanced options.
- **Skill Development**
    - **Learning About Nutrition**: Teaching about the importance of different food groups in a way that is accessible.
    - **Culinary Skills**: Building confidence and independence in preparing meals.

a. **Behavioral Strategies**

- **Positive Reinforcement**
    - **Encouragement**: Praising attempts to try new foods or engage in

mealtime routines.

- ○ **Rewards Systems**: Implementing a system where trying new foods leads to earned privileges or activities.

- **Modeling Behavior**
  - ○ **Demonstration**: Caregivers and peers modeling enjoyable eating experiences.
  - ○ **Peer Interaction**: Encouraging social meals with understanding friends who can provide positive influence.

a. Addressing Emotional and Psychological Factors

- **Anxiety Management**
  - ○ **Relaxation Techniques**: Breathing exercises or mindfulness practices before meals.
  - ○ **Therapeutic Support**: Working with a psychologist or counselor to address underlying anxieties.
- **Cognitive Behavioral Approaches**
  - ○ **Challenging Negative Thoughts**: Identifying and reframing thoughts that contribute to food avoidance.
  - ○ **Setting Realistic Goals**: Establishing achievable objectives to gradually expand food preferences.

a. Professional Interventions

- **Occupational Therapy**
  - ○ **Sensory Integration Therapy**: Techniques to help the individual process sensory information more effectively.
  - ○ **Feeding Therapy**: Specific interventions aimed at improving eating behaviors.
- **Dietary Consultation**
  - ○ **Nutritionists and Dietitians**: Professionals can create meal plans that meet nutritional needs while respecting sensory preferences.
- **Medical Evaluation**
  - ○ **Assessing for Underlying Conditions**: Rule out medical issues that may contribute to eating challenges, such as gastrointestinal disorders.

a. **Support for Families and Caregivers**

- **Education and Training**
  - ○ **Understanding Sensory Processing**: Learning about sensory differences to better support the individual.
  - ○ **Effective Communication**: Strategies for discussing food-related issues without causing stress.
- **Resource Utilization**
  - ○ **Support Groups**: Connecting with other families facing similar challenges.
  - ○ **Professional Guidance**: Seeking advice from specialists in autism and eating behaviors.

Personal perspectives and expert advice (e.g., Jess Hendrickx's story)

Gaining insights from those who have firsthand experience with eating and sensory sensitivities can provide valuable understanding and practical tips. Personal stories and expert opinions highlight the diversity of experiences and emphasize the importance of individualized approaches.

a. **Personal Narratives**

- **Experiences of Autistic Women**
  - ○ **Challenges Faced**
    - ▪ **Isolation**: Feeling misunderstood or judged due to eating behaviors.
    - ▪ **Trial and Error**: The process of discovering which strategies work best can be lengthy.
  - ○ **Success Stories**
    - ▪ **Overcoming Barriers**: Accounts of individuals who have expanded their diets and improved their relationships with food.
    - ▪ **Self-Advocacy**: Empowering oneself by communicating needs and preferences to others.

- **Impact on Daily Life**
  - **Social Situations**: Navigating events like parties or dining out can be stressful but manageable with planning.
  - **Emotional Growth**: Increased confidence and self-esteem as challenges are addressed.

a. **Expert Opinions**

- **Jess Hendrickx's Story**
  - **Background**
    - **Who is Jess Hendrickx?** An autistic advocate and professional specializing in autism and mental health.
    - **Contributions**: Shares personal experiences and professional insights to help others understand and manage sensory sensitivities.
  - **Key Insights**
    - **Acceptance**: Emphasizes accepting one's sensory differences rather than trying to conform to neurotypical standards.
    - **Tailored Strategies**: Advocates for individualized approaches that consider the person's unique sensory profile.
- **Other Professionals**
  - **Occupational Therapists**
    - **Role**: Assist in developing practical strategies for sensory management.
    - **Advice**: Importance of early intervention and consistent practice.
  - **Dietitians Specialized in Autism**
    - **Nutritional Balance**: Focus on ensuring dietary needs are met despite restrictions.
    - **Collaboration**: Working closely with individuals and families to create sustainable eating plans.

a. **Common Themes and Lessons Learned**

- **Flexibility and Patience**

- ○ **Gradual Progress**: Recognizing that change takes time and small steps are valuable.
  - ○ **Adapting Strategies**: Being willing to modify approaches as needed.
- **Communication is Key**
  - ○ **Open Dialogue**: Encouraging honest discussions about preferences and challenges.
  - ○ **Advocacy**: Teaching individuals to express their needs confidently.
- **Emphasis on Well-Being Over Conformity**
  - ○ **Personal Comfort**: Prioritizing strategies that enhance comfort and reduce stress.
  - ○ **Rejecting Pressure**: Avoiding forcing changes that cause distress or are unsustainable.

a. **Resources and Support Networks**

- **Books and Publications**
  - ○ **Recommended Reading**: Titles that provide further insight into managing eating and sensory sensitivities.
- **Online Communities**
  - ○ **Forums and Social Media Groups**: Platforms where individuals can share experiences and advice.
- **Professional Organizations**
  - ○ **Autism Associations**: Offer resources, workshops, and connections to specialists.

a. **Encouraging a Holistic Approach**

- **Integrating Physical and Mental Health**
  - ○ **Mind-Body Connection**: Understanding how emotional well-being affects eating behaviors.
  - ○ **Consistent Care**: Coordinating between different professionals for comprehensive support.
- **Family and Community Involvement**
  - ○ **Collaborative Efforts**: Involving family members, educators, and peers in supporting the individual's needs.

    ◦ **Promoting Understanding**: Educating others to reduce stigma and foster acceptance.

Self-Advocacy and Community Building

Advocacy and community support play pivotal roles in enhancing the lives of autistic women and girls. By raising awareness, challenging misconceptions, and fostering inclusive environments, advocacy efforts contribute to social change and empower individuals to embrace their identities fully. Community support networks provide essential resources, connections, and a sense of belonging, which are crucial for personal growth and well-being. This chapter explores the importance of self-advocacy, the impact of broader advocacy movements, and the ways in which community support can be cultivated and accessed.

Empowering autistic women to advocate for themselves

Self-advocacy involves understanding one's own needs and effectively communicating them to others. For autistic women, this skill is crucial in overcoming barriers and achieving personal and professional goals.

a. **Understanding Self-Advocacy**

- **Defining Self-Advocacy**
    - ◦ **Personal Agency**: Recognizing one's right to make choices about one's own life.
    - ◦ **Communication**: Effectively expressing needs, desires, and rights.
- **Importance of Self-Advocacy**
    - ◦ **Empowerment**: Builds confidence and independence.
    - ◦ **Access to Resources**: Ensures appropriate accommodations and support are received.
    - ◦ **Influencing Change**: Personal advocacy can lead to broader societal shifts.

a. **Developing Self-Awareness**

- **Identifying Strengths and Challenges**

- ○ **Strengths**: Acknowledge areas of strong ability, such as attention to detail or creativity.
  - ○ **Challenges**: Recognize areas where support is needed, like sensory sensitivities or social communication.
- **Understanding Personal Needs**
  - ○ **Sensory Needs**: Know what sensory inputs are overwhelming or calming.
  - ○ **Communication Preferences**: Determine the most comfortable ways to communicate (e.g., written, verbal, visual aids).

a. **Building Communication Skills**

- **Effective Communication Strategies**
  - ○ **Clarity**: Use clear and concise language.
  - ○ **Assertiveness**: Express needs confidently without aggression.
  - ○ **Active Listening**: Practice listening to others to enhance mutual understanding.
- **Utilizing Tools and Aids**
  - ○ **Visual Supports**: Use charts, diagrams, or apps to convey information.
  - ○ **Scripts and Rehearsals**: Prepare for conversations by practicing scenarios.

a. **Navigating Different Environments**

- **Educational Settings**
  - ○ **Accommodations**: Request necessary support, such as extended time on tests or sensory-friendly spaces.
  - ○ **Collaboration with Educators**: Work with teachers to create an optimal learning environment.
- **Workplace Advocacy**
  - ○ **Disclosure Decisions**: Weigh the pros and cons of disclosing autism to employers.
  - ○ **Requesting Accommodations**: Communicate specific needs, like flexible scheduling or modified workspaces.

a. **Overcoming Internal Barriers**

- **Building Confidence**
    - ○ **Positive Self-Talk**: Replace negative thoughts with affirming statements.
    - ○ **Celebrating Successes**: Acknowledge and reward personal achievements.
- **Managing Anxiety and Fear**
    - ○ **Relaxation Techniques**: Practice deep breathing or mindfulness exercises.
    - ○ **Support Networks**: Rely on friends, family, or mentors for encouragement.

a. **Learning and Knowing Rights**

- **Legal Knowledge**
    - ○ **Disability Rights**: Familiarize with laws like the Americans with Disabilities Act (ADA).
    - ○ **Educational Rights**: Understand entitlements under the Individuals with Disabilities Education Act (IDEA).
- **Advocacy Resources**
    - ○ **Workshops and Seminars**: Attend events focused on self-advocacy skills.
    - ○ **Online Platforms**: Utilize websites and forums dedicated to autism advocacy.

Building and participating in supportive networks

Supportive networks offer emotional assistance, share resources, and create a sense of community. Participation in these networks can significantly enhance the quality of life for autistic women.

a. **Finding the Right Community**

- **Identifying Needs and Interests**
    - ○ **Common Interests**: Seek groups that align with personal hobbies or passions.

- **Shared Experiences**: Find communities specifically for autistic women.
- **Types of Support Networks**
  - **Local Groups**: In-person meetups, workshops, or social events.
  - **Online Communities**: Forums, social media groups, or virtual support networks.

a. Benefits of Supportive Networks

- **Emotional Support**
  - **Understanding**: Connect with others who share similar experiences.
  - **Validation**: Feelings and challenges are acknowledged and respected.
- **Resource Sharing**
  - **Information Exchange**: Learn about coping strategies, accommodations, and services.
  - **Opportunities**: Access to events, workshops, or job openings.

a. Participating Effectively

- **Engagement Strategies**
  - **Active Participation**: Attend meetings regularly and contribute to discussions.
  - **Volunteering**: Offer skills or time to support group activities.
- **Communication Etiquette**
  - **Respectful Interaction**: Practice empathy and consider others' perspectives.
  - **Boundaries**: Set and respect personal limits in social interactions.

a. Building Your Own Network

- **Starting a Group**
  - **Identify a Need**: Determine if there's a gap in available support networks.
  - **Logistics**: Plan meeting locations, times, and formats (in-person or virtual).
- **Promoting Inclusivity**
  - **Diversity**: Encourage participation from individuals of various

backgrounds.

- ○ **Accessibility**: Ensure meetings are sensory-friendly and accommodate different communication styles.

a. Leveraging Technology

- **Online Platforms**
  - ○ **Social Media**: Use Facebook groups, Twitter, or Instagram to connect.
  - ○ **Dedicated Apps**: Explore apps designed for community building and support.
- **Virtual Events**
  - ○ **Webinars and Workshops**: Attend or host online educational sessions.
  - ○ **Virtual Meetups**: Use video conferencing tools for real-time interaction.

a. Sustaining Networks

- **Regular Communication**
  - ○ **Newsletters**: Share updates, stories, and resources.
  - ○ **Group Chats**: Maintain ongoing conversations through messaging apps.
- **Feedback and Adaptation**
  - ○ **Solicit Input**: Encourage members to share ideas for improvement.
  - ○ **Flexibility**: Adapt to the evolving needs of the community.

The role of allies, advocates, and professionals

Allies, advocates, and professionals play crucial roles in supporting autistic women and enhancing their advocacy efforts.

a. Understanding the Role of Allies

- **Who Are Allies?**
  - ○ **Friends and Family**: Individuals close to the autistic person who provide support.
  - ○ **Colleagues and Acquaintances**: People in the wider social circle who promote understanding.
- **Responsibilities of Allies**

- **Listening and Learning**: Actively seek to understand autistic experiences.
- **Advocating Respectfully**: Support without overshadowing the voices of autistic individuals.
- **Challenging Misconceptions**: Address stereotypes and misinformation.

a. The Impact of Advocates

- **Professional Advocates**
  - **Legal Advocates**: Assist with navigating legal rights and discrimination cases.
  - **Educational Advocates**: Support in securing appropriate educational accommodations.
- **Peer Advocates**
  - **Mentorship**: Provide guidance based on personal experiences.
  - **Role Models**: Inspire others by demonstrating successful advocacy.

a. Professionals in Support

- **Healthcare Providers**
  - **Understanding Practitioners**: Offer compassionate care and recognize unique needs.
  - **Therapists and Counselors**: Provide strategies for coping and personal development.
- **Educators**
  - **Inclusive Teaching**: Implement teaching methods that accommodate different learning styles.
  - **Supportive Environment**: Foster a classroom culture that values diversity.

a. Collaboration Between Autistic Women and Allies

- **Effective Partnerships**
  - **Open Communication**: Share goals, challenges, and expectations.
  - **Mutual Respect**: Acknowledge each person's expertise and perspective.

- **Advocacy Initiatives**
    - ○ **Joint Campaigns**: Collaborate on projects promoting awareness and inclusion.
    - ○ **Educational Programs**: Develop resources or workshops together.

a. Encouraging Allyship

- **Education and Awareness**
    - ○ **Training Programs**: Allies can participate in sensitivity training or autism education.
    - ○ **Resource Sharing**: Provide materials that help allies understand autism better.
- **Active Involvement**
    - ○ **Support Groups**: Allies can attend meetings to learn and offer support.
    - ○ **Community Events**: Participate in events that promote inclusion.

a. Professional Development for Support Roles

- **Continuous Learning**
    - ○ **Staying Informed**: Keep up-to-date with the latest research and best practices.
    - ○ **Cultural Competence**: Understand how intersectionality affects autistic women.
- **Ethical Practice**
    - ○ **Empowerment Focus**: Professionals should aim to empower rather than control.
    - ○ **Consent and Autonomy**: Respect the decisions and independence of autistic individuals.

Part VI: Thriving as an Autistic Woman

Living Well in a Non-Autistic World

Living in a world primarily designed for neurotypical individuals presents unique challenges for autistic women. However, by overcoming societal barriers, celebrating personal strengths, and building an authentic life, autistic women can not only navigate but thrive in this environment. This chapter explores strategies for addressing misconceptions, recognizing and leveraging individual achievements, and creating a fulfilling life that honors one's true self.

Overcoming societal barriers and misconceptions

Societal barriers and misconceptions about autism can impede personal and professional growth. Challenging these obstacles is essential for fostering acceptance and inclusion.

a. **Identifying Common Misconceptions**

- **Stereotypes About Autism**
  - **Homogeneity Myth:** Belief that all autistic individuals are the same.
  - **Lack of Empathy:** Misconception that autistic people cannot feel or express empathy.
  - **Social Disinterest:** Assumption that autistic individuals do not desire social connections.
- **Gender-Specific Misconceptions**
  - **Underdiagnosis in Women:** Ignorance of how autism presents differently in females.
  - **Behavioral Expectations:** Societal pressures for women to conform to certain social norms.

a. **Strategies for Overcoming Barriers**

- **Education and Awareness**
  - **Personal Advocacy:** Share personal experiences to educate others.
  - **Public Speaking and Writing:** Engage in outreach through blogs,

articles, or talks.

- **Challenging Stereotypes**
  - ○ **Demonstrating Diversity**: Highlight the varied experiences and abilities within the autistic community.
  - ○ **Correcting Misinformation**: Address inaccuracies when encountered in conversations or media.
- **Legal and Policy Advocacy**
  - ○ **Know Your Rights**: Understand legal protections against discrimination.
  - ○ **Engage in Policy Change**: Participate in advocacy groups aiming to influence legislation.

a. **Building Resilience**

- **Developing Coping Mechanisms**
  - ○ **Stress Management**: Techniques such as mindfulness, exercise, or creative outlets.
  - ○ **Support Systems**: Rely on trusted friends, family, or professionals during challenging times.
- **Positive Mindset**
  - ○ **Focus on Strengths**: Concentrate on abilities rather than limitations.
  - ○ **Set Realistic Goals**: Create achievable objectives to foster a sense of accomplishment.

Celebrating strengths and achievements

Recognizing and valuing one's unique strengths is crucial for self-esteem and motivation. Autistic women possess diverse talents that contribute significantly to various fields.

a. **Identifying Personal Strengths**

- **Self-Reflection**
  - ○ **Journaling**: Write about skills, achievements, and areas of interest.
  - ○ **Feedback from Others**: Seek input from trusted individuals who can provide insight.

- **Strength Assessment Tools**
  - ° **Personality Tests**: Utilize assessments like the Myers-Briggs Type Indicator (MBTI) to understand traits.
  - ° **Professional Guidance**: Work with coaches or therapists to identify strengths.

a. **Leveraging Strengths in Various Areas**

- **Career Development**
  - ° **Specialized Skills**: Apply talents in roles that value attention to detail, creativity, or analytical thinking.
  - ° **Continuous Learning**: Pursue further education or training in areas of interest.
- **Personal Relationships**
  - ° **Authenticity**: Build relationships based on genuine interests and mutual respect.
  - ° **Communication**: Use preferred communication styles to strengthen connections.

a. **Celebrating Achievements**

- **Acknowledgment**
  - ° **Personal Recognition**: Take time to acknowledge successes, big or small.
  - ° **Sharing Milestones**: Celebrate achievements with others to enhance joy and encouragement.
- **Reward Systems**
  - ° **Personal Rewards**: Treat oneself after reaching goals as motivation.
  - ° **Public Recognition**: Accept praise and awards graciously.

Building a fulfilling and authentic life

Creating a life that aligns with one's values and preferences is key to long-term happiness and satisfaction.

a. **Defining Personal Values and Goals**

- **Values Clarification**
  - ◦ **Core Beliefs**: Identify what matters most, such as honesty, creativity, or independence.
  - ◦ **Prioritization**: Determine which values take precedence when making decisions.
- **Goal Setting**
  - ◦ **Short-Term Goals**: Set immediate objectives that are attainable.
  - ◦ **Long-Term Vision**: Outline aspirations for the future, considering personal and professional domains.

a. **Creating an Authentic Lifestyle**

- **Honoring Preferences**
  - ◦ **Living Environment**: Design spaces that cater to sensory needs and comfort.
  - ◦ **Daily Routine**: Establish routines that provide structure and flexibility.
- **Pursuing Passions**
  - ◦ **Hobbies and Interests**: Dedicate time to activities that bring joy and fulfillment.
  - ◦ **Community Involvement**: Engage with groups or causes that resonate with personal values.

a. **Fostering Healthy Relationships**

- **Quality Over Quantity**
  - ◦ **Selective Socialization**: Choose relationships that are supportive and enriching.
  - ◦ **Boundaries**: Set and maintain boundaries to protect well-being.
- **Effective Communication**
  - ◦ **Expressing Needs**: Clearly articulate expectations and feelings.
  - ◦ **Active Listening**: Practice attentive listening to strengthen connections.

a. **Self-Care and Well-Being**

- **Physical Health**

- **Nutrition**: Maintain a balanced diet accommodating sensory preferences.
  - **Exercise**: Incorporate physical activity suited to individual abilities and interests.
- **Mental Health**
  - **Therapeutic Support**: Seek professional help when needed.
  - **Relaxation Techniques**: Use methods like meditation or deep breathing to manage stress.

a. Adapting to Change

- **Flexibility**
  - **Embracing Growth**: View change as an opportunity for development.
  - **Coping Strategies**: Develop plans to manage unexpected events.
- **Continuous Learning**
  - **Skill Development**: Pursue new skills that enhance personal or professional life.
  - **Open-Mindedness**: Stay receptive to new ideas and perspectives.

Stories from Autistic Women

The experiences of autistic women are rich, varied, and deeply insightful. Sharing these stories not only empowers those who tell them but also provides guidance and inspiration to others navigating similar paths. This chapter brings together personal narratives, lessons learned, and messages of resilience and hope from autistic women around the world.

Personal narratives and insights

a. Emma's Journey: From Misdiagnosis to Self-Discovery

- **Early Childhood and Misdiagnosis**
  - **Struggling in Silence**

Emma, growing up in a small town, always felt different. She was hypersensitive to sounds and textures, often overwhelmed by environments that others found normal.

- **Misdiagnosed with Anxiety and Depression**

Without awareness of autism in girls, Emma was diagnosed with anxiety and depression during her teenage years. Traditional treatments provided little relief.

- **The Turning Point**
  - **Discovering Autism**

At 28, Emma stumbled upon an article about autism in women. The descriptions resonated deeply, prompting her to seek a reassessment.

- **Receiving the Correct Diagnosis**

Undergoing evaluation with a specialist familiar with autism in adult women led to an accurate diagnosis, bringing clarity to her lifelong experiences.

- **Embracing Her Identity**
  - **Self-Education**

Immersing herself in literature about autism, Emma began to understand her sensory sensitivities and social challenges.

- **Connecting with the Community**

Joining online forums and local support groups allowed her to share experiences and feel less isolated.

b. Maya's Career Path: Thriving in the Tech Industry

- **Educational Pursuits**

- ○ **Passion for Technology**

Maya excelled in mathematics and computer science, finding solace in the logical structures of programming languages.

- **Challenges in University**

Group projects and networking events were daunting due to social communication difficulties.

- **Navigating the Workplace**
  - ○ **Securing Her First Job**

Landing a position as a software developer, Maya initially struggled with office politics and unstructured team meetings.

- **Implementing Coping Strategies**

She developed strategies like preparing scripts for meetings and using project management tools to communicate preferences.

- **Advocacy and Mentorship**
  - ○ **Promoting Neurodiversity at Work**

Maya initiated a neurodiversity program within her company, educating colleagues and management about autism.

- **Mentoring Others**

She mentors young autistic professionals, helping them navigate the tech industry.

c. Sofia's Story: Balancing Parenthood and Personal Needs

- **Family Life**
  - ○ **Raising an Autistic Child**

Sofia's son was diagnosed with autism at age 4, prompting her to reflect on her own experiences.

- **Pursuing Her Diagnosis**

Recognizing similarities, Sofia sought an assessment and was diagnosed with autism herself.

- **Personal Growth**
  - **Understanding Her Past**

The diagnosis helped Sofia make sense of past struggles, including sensory overload and social anxiety.

- **Implementing Self-Care**

She began prioritizing self-care routines, such as scheduling quiet time and engaging in her love for painting.

- **Community Involvement**
  - **Advocacy Work**

Sofia became active in advocating for better support services in schools for autistic children.

- **Creating Support Networks**

She established a local group for autistic parents, providing a platform for shared experiences and resources.

Lessons learned and advice for others on the spectrum

a. **Embracing Self-Acceptance**

- **Understanding Yourself**
  - **Self-Reflection Practices**

Engage in journaling or mindfulness to explore personal feelings and reactions.

- **Identifying Strengths**

Make a list of personal strengths, talents, and interests to build confidence.

- **Letting Go of Societal Expectations**
  - **Redefining Success**

Define what success means personally, rather than adhering to societal norms.

- **Accepting Limitations**

Recognize that it's okay to have limitations and to seek assistance when needed.

a. **Navigating Social Relationships**

- **Building Authentic Connections**
  - **Quality Over Quantity**

Focus on nurturing a few deep relationships rather than numerous superficial ones.

- **Shared Interests**

Join clubs or groups centered around hobbies to meet like-minded people.

- **Effective Communication**
  - **Expressing Needs Clearly**

Practice stating needs and preferences directly to avoid misunderstandings.

- **Active Listening**

Show engagement in conversations by summarizing what others have said and asking follow-up questions.

a. **Managing Mental Health**

- **Recognizing Signs of Overwhelm**
    - **Physical Indicators**

Pay attention to signs like fatigue, headaches, or changes in sleep patterns.

- **Emotional Cues**

Notice feelings of irritability, anxiety, or depression as signals to take a step back.

- **Implementing Coping Strategies**
    - **Mindfulness and Relaxation**

Incorporate activities like yoga, meditation, or deep-breathing exercises into daily routines.

- **Professional Support**

Seek therapists or counselors experienced in working with autistic individuals.

a. **Pursuing Personal and Professional Goals**

- **Setting Achievable Objectives**
    - **Specific Planning**

Use goal-setting frameworks to outline steps toward personal or career aspirations.

- **Flexibility**

Allow room for adjustments as interests and circumstances evolve.

- **Leveraging Support Systems**
    - **Mentorship**

Connect with mentors in desired fields who can provide guidance and encouragement.

- **Networking**

Attend events or join professional organizations to expand opportunities.

Inspiring resilience and hope

a. Overcoming Adversity

- **Personal Triumphs**
    - **Educational Achievements**

Stories of women returning to education after obstacles and achieving degrees.

- **Entrepreneurial Successes**

Autistic women starting their own businesses, turning passions into livelihoods.

- **Community Impact**
    - **Advocacy Initiatives**

Examples of grassroots movements led by autistic women resulting in policy changes.

- **Creative Contributions**

Artists, writers, and musicians sharing their talents and gaining recognition.

b. Messages of Encouragement

- **Belief in Self**
    - **Affirmations**

"Your differences are your strengths."

- **Perseverance**

"Challenges are stepping stones to growth."

- **Building a Supportive Future**
    - **Collective Effort**

Emphasizing the importance of community in fostering acceptance and understanding.

- **Inspiring Others**

Encouraging sharing of stories to empower and educate.

The Future of Autism in Women and Girls

As society progresses toward greater understanding and inclusivity, the future for autistic women and girls holds promise. Advances in research, increased awareness, and proactive advocacy are shaping a world that recognizes and values neurodiversity. This chapter explores efforts to promote inclusion, highlights significant advancements in diagnosis and support, and envisions a better future for upcoming generations.

Promoting inclusion and understanding

a. Educational Initiatives

- **Inclusive Curricula**
  - **Neurodiversity Education**

Integrate lessons on neurodiversity into school programs to foster acceptance from a young age.

- **Teacher Training**

Provide educators with resources and training to support autistic students effectively.

- **Awareness Campaigns**
  - **Community Workshops**

Host events that educate the public about autism in women and girls, dispelling myths and stereotypes.

- **Media Engagement**

Encourage accurate and positive representation of autistic women in media outlets.

b. Workplace Diversity and Inclusion

- **Employer Education**
  - **Training Programs**

Develop workshops for employers on the benefits of neurodiverse workplaces and how to support autistic employees.

- **Policy Development**

Implement inclusive hiring practices and reasonable accommodation policies.

- **Supportive Employment Models**
    - **Job Coaching**

Offer personalized support to help autistic women navigate workplace challenges.

- **Flexible Work Arrangements**

Provide options like remote work, flexible hours, or adjusted workloads to accommodate individual needs.

c. Community Engagement

- **Building Support Networks**
    - **Local Support Groups**

Establish groups that provide resources and a sense of community for autistic women and their families.

- **Online Platforms**

Expand digital communities that offer support, information, and connection regardless of geographical location.

- **Advocacy and Representation**
    - **Involving Autistic Voices**

Ensure autistic women are represented in decision-making processes that affect their lives.

- **Public Policy Influence**

Advocate for legislation that protects the rights and improves services for autistic individuals.

Advances in research and diagnosis

a. Gender-Sensitive Diagnostic Tools

- **Revising Diagnostic Criteria**
    - **Inclusion of Female Presentation**

Update diagnostic manuals to reflect how autism manifests differently in women and girls.

- **Development of New Assessments**

Create screening tools specifically designed to identify autism in females.

- **Early Intervention**
    - **Pediatric Training**

Educate pediatricians to recognize early signs of autism in girls.

- **Parental Guidance**

Provide resources to help parents understand developmental milestones and seek assessments when necessary.

b. Research on Biological and Environmental Factors

- **Neurological Studies**
    - **Brain Imaging**

Utilize advanced imaging techniques to study neurological patterns associated with autism in females.

- **Hormonal Influences**

Investigate the role of hormones in the development and expression of autistic traits.

- **Genetic Research**
    - **Gene Identification**

Explore genetic markers that may be linked to autism in women.

- **Epigenetics**

Study how environmental factors may affect gene expression related to autism.

c. Innovations in Support Services

- **Personalized Intervention Programs**
    - **Tailored Therapies**

Develop interventions that consider individual sensory profiles, communication styles, and learning preferences.

- **Technology-Assisted Support**

Use apps and assistive devices to enhance communication and daily functioning.

- **Integrated Care Models**
    - **Multidisciplinary Teams**

Coordinate care among professionals like psychologists, occupational therapists, and educators.

- **Family Involvement**

Include family members in planning and implementing support strategies.

Shaping a better world for future generations

a. Policy and Legislation

- **Strengthening Legal Protections**
    - **Anti-Discrimination Laws**

Advocate for robust enforcement of laws protecting autistic individuals from discrimination.

- **Accessibility Regulations**

Ensure public spaces and services are accessible to those with sensory sensitivities.

- **Global Collaboration**
    - **International Agreements**

Participate in global initiatives to standardize support and rights for autistic individuals worldwide.

- **Sharing Best Practices**

Exchange successful programs and policies between countries to improve global support.

b. Cultural Transformation

- **Changing Perceptions**
    - **Media Representation**

Promote diverse and accurate portrayals of autistic women in media.

- **Public Discourse**

Encourage open conversations about neurodiversity to reduce stigma.

- **Celebrating Neurodiversity**
    - **Community Events**

Organize festivals, art exhibitions, and conferences that highlight the talents of autistic individuals.

- **Education Campaigns**

Launch initiatives that educate the public about the value of neurodiversity.

c. Empowering the Next Generation

- **Youth Programs**
    - **Mentorship Opportunities**

Connect young autistic girls with mentors who can provide guidance and support.

- **Leadership Development**

Offer programs that build confidence and leadership skills.

- **Technological Advancements**
    - **Assistive Technologies**

Invest in developing tools that enhance communication and learning.

- **Accessible Education Platforms**

Create online learning environments that accommodate different learning styles and needs.

Special Thanks

To Our Valued Readers,

We extend our deepest gratitude to each and every one of you who have purchased and read this book. Your curiosity, openness, and commitment to understanding the unique experiences of autistic women and girls make a profound difference. By choosing to engage with these stories and insights, you are contributing to a more inclusive and compassionate world.

Your support not only empowers those on the spectrum but also encourages continued dialogue, learning, and advocacy. We hope that this book has provided valuable perspectives, sparked meaningful conversations, and perhaps even inspired personal or communal growth.

Thank you for being a vital part of this journey toward greater awareness, acceptance, and celebration of neurodiversity. Your willingness to listen and learn brings us all one step closer to a world where every individual is recognized and valued for who they are.

With heartfelt appreciation,

Layane Miled

Also by Layane Miled

Her Spectrum: The Unique Journey of Women and Girls with Autism